CULTURE PATTERNS
IN CHRISTIANITY

Wilson D. Wallis

CULTURE PATTERNS
IN CHRISTIANITY

With the Collaboration of

John E. Longhurst

Coronado Press   1972

Second Printing: July, 1972
SBN 87291—053—9

Manufactured in the USA

To Omer C. Stewart

*Ye shall know the truth,
and the truth shall make you free.*

PREFACE

This book is to some extent a brief account of Christianity as a historic phenomenon. The emphasis is on responses to influences from other (non-Christian) sources, not on its development in response to them. Hence, in this sense, Christianity has of necessity always been a development from within. Being influenced by the culture in which it flourishes, it must, to a degree, be a child of time and place. Otherwise it is not intelligible; and even if intelligible, it cannot be appealing. For receptivity implies understanding, and to have meaning for its recipients, a message must be in a language which is comprehensible.

We do not presume to assess the religious significance, but merely the culture influences — the adoptions and adaptations — which have appeared in Christianity from time to time. Our role is that of observer and recorder, not that of a critic or an evaluator.

My obligations to the Editor for assistance and advice manifold and abundant, far exceed the usual indebtedness of author to editor.

W.D.W.

South Woodstock, Connecticut
June 1, 1964

CONTENTS

CHAPTER ONE

Christianity in Culture

OLIVER Wendell Holmes said, in 1859: "Our religion has been Judaized; it has been Romanized; it has been orientalized; it has been Anglicized; and the time is at hand when it must be Americanized. Every age has to shape the Divine image it worships over again—the present age and all our own country are busily engaged in the task at this time." Many centuries before, Clement of Alexandria referred to Christianity as a river which receives tributaries from all sides. And, indeed, Christianity has been shaped and influenced in many ways by the cultures through which it has passed. It is indebted to Dionysian myth, Greek philosophy, Jewish messianism, Iranian Zoroastrianism. It developed in lands of the Mediterranean at a time of cultural diffusion from Egypt to the eastern Mediterranean and Persia, and from the eastern Mediterranean to Scandinavia and the British Isles. Amid these influences, in a world of widening contacts, Christianity was cradled. If the new religion was to grow in stature and influence, it must breathe the atmosphere of this larger world.

It is no surprise, then, to find that the New Testament contains borrowings from Hellenistic, Roman and Iranian cultures. As Christianity spread it adopted

concepts and practices from other religions with
which it came into contact. An episode in the life of
Bishop Gregory, of ancient times, originally recorded
by the historian Eusebius and repeated in medieval
times by John of Salisbury, illustrates the relations
of the early Christian church with paganism. "The
blessed Gregory, bishop of Gneocesarea," writes John
of Salisbury,[1] "overtaken in the Alps by night and a
storm, stopped at a shrine of Apollo, who is revered
by the natives of the neighborhood. He was enter-
tained most courteously by the officiating priest,
though he was a heathen. Mindful of his courteous
reception and at the request of the priest he freed
Apollo from the ban by which he had deprived him of
the right of delivering oracles and mocking the spirits
of the dead. The facts given in greater detail may be
found in the *Ecclesiastical History* of Eusebius of
Cesarea. On his authority it is established that the
priest pursued with laments the blessed Gregory,
charging him with ingratitude and complaining that
his courtesy had been inadequately repaid. The holy
man gave him the following note to take back to the
god Apollo: 'Gregory to Apollo: I permit thee to
return to thy place and to engage in thy accustomed
activities.' After the priest had delivered the note to
the idol, the demon being released, began in his usual
way to practise deception with his oracles. Consequently the priest, amazed at the majesty of Him
whose humble servants could in this way hold sway
over pagan gods and suspend and torture with a word,
turned in scorn from his Apollo, and following Gregory,

[1] In *Policraticus*, Book VIII.

became his adherent. He who had been priest of Apollo turned apostle of Christ and made such progress in faith and religion that he is believed to have succeeded the blessed Gregory as head of the church of Gneocesarea. Thus the hospitality of the priest was rewarded first by worldly preferment and finally by heavenly salvation."

Christianity has responded to a variety of social influences and its history is one of constant change and adaptation from century to century and region to region. Even before the end of the first century Christianity had assumed regionally distinctive characteristics, some of which have persisted to the present day. It has likewise been modified—in ideology, theology, ritual, symbolism, regalia, architecture and sacred history—in other regions, such as Ethiopia, Syria, India and Latin America. In Europe proper the schism of 718 resulted in a doctrinal and regional division between Eastern Church and Western Church, which division still exists: west of the Adriatic is the Western, or Roman Catholic Church with its Protestant offspring; to the east is the Orthodox, or Eastern Church. After the Protestant Reformation of the sixteenth century, southwest Europe remains Roman Catholic, while northwest Europe becomes Protestant. Germany divides between South (Catholic) and North (Protestant). Ireland remains Catholic and the rest of the British Isles turns to Protestantism. The northern European states, principally Germanic in speech, are predominantly Protestant, whereas the Latin countries (except Rumania), the Baltic states of Lithuania and Latvia, and the Slavic areas of western Europe, adhere to Catholicism. The remainder of Slavic Europe for the most part continues its allegiance to the Orthodox, or Eastern Catholic, church.

Egyptian Influences

The Egyptian concept of the weighing of the soul of the deceased, which influenced Christian ideology, probably by way of India or Iran, is referred to in *Daniel*: "Thou art weighed in the balances and art found wanting." This concept is represented realistically in medieval ecclesiastic art. A bas-relief in a church in Velay (France) depicts an angel weighing souls, and the devil, in the form of a pig—an Egyptian touch—carrying away a woman whose virtue, or virtues, have been found wanting. Meanwhile the devil keeps an eye on the scales to see that the angel does not cheat him of the remainder of the ponderable wares. In a thirteenth-century church sculpture at Louques the devil slyly touches the beam with a finger to cause the scales to incline in his favor. In a stained-glass window of the cathedral of Bourges he puts his foot on the scales and presses the lever with his right hand, while one of his imps pulls at it from below, so as to cause virtue to kick the beam. The careful provisions which the ancient Egyptians made to assure impartial judgment were apparently not typical of Christianity in the middle ages.

The use of scales in assessing justice appears in an old legend about a man who had aided another whose wagon had turned over on him and imprisoned him in the mud. When the soul of the benefactor—who happened to be a rich man—appeared for judgment before the Heavenly Tribunal, the Angelic Prosecutor indicted him for his many sins. The Scales of Justice tipped dangerously toward Gehenna; the outcome looked bad for him until "the Angel of Mercy entered and demanded of the Eternal Judge that the man's good deed be weighed against his sins." When these good deeds were put into the scales, they "tipped toward Paradise."

The white linen robes of Egyptian priests inspired the white vestments used in Christian worship. It is also possible that the rule requiring women to be veiled during the Isis ceremonies accounts for the Christian requirement—also an ancient Greek custom at temples—that the woman's head be covered in a church.

During the ancient Egyptian celebration of the Resurrection of Osiris, lamps were lighted and brought in at the Twelfth Hour. The doors were then closed, Osiris was purified by Horus, and the gods watching at the bier shouted: "Hail to thee, God! Hail to thee, Soul of the gods!" The early Christians forbade the use of candles in church services, alleging (correctly) that this was a pagan practice. However, by the end of the third century many churches were using candles during service, and the custom continued thereafter.

Herodotus describes an annual Egyptian festival at which Rhampsinitus, an unidentified god or king, descended into Hell and returned to earth. At this probably Osirian festival the priests wrapped a man in a shroud, led him beyond the city to a temple of Isis, and left him there. Two priests, in the role of divine guides for the dead, led him back; with him, he carried a napkin, given to him in the underworld.

In *John* , a late Gospel, those who went to the tomb of Jesus saw the napkin lying in one place, the shroud in another, and two celestial figures nearby—a description strongly suggestive of Egyptian ceremony.

Isis myths influenced the cult of Mary, Mother of God, and assisted in elevating her to a celestial position. In thousands of statuary and paintings, Isis, mother of Horus, holds the divine child in her arms. Christianity adopted these statues and pictures to represent the Madonna and Child. Christian representations are such exact duplicates of the Egyptian that he is a wise archeologist who knows whose mother and child are represented—whether Isis and Horus, or Mary and Jesus. Isis was later identified with Diana, or Artemis, and Mary was gradually substituted for Artemis. Both Isis and Artemis (the latter under the name of Selene) were identified with the moon and were symbolized by a crescent, which accounts for the presence of a crescent moon in many paintings of the Virgin Mary.

Isis was also identified with Aphrodite, who was born of the foam of the sea and came to be the patron goddess of the sea and seamen. After the Madonna had been identified with Isis, or had replaced her, she was called *Stella Maris*, "Star of the Sea," and is often so designated in Roman Catholic countries.

The cathedral at Aix, in France, contains a figure of Isis holding a ship in her hand, carved, in medieval times, in an ivory panel in the side of the ambo, or pulpit. A statue of Isis adorned a pillar in the Cologne church of St. Ursula in the middle ages.

In the church of St. Germain-des-Prés, which was built on the ruins of a temple of Isis around the middle of the sixth century, a statue of the ancient goddess was transferred to the new edifice where it was worshiped for nearly ten centuries until it was destroyed in 1514. A village church near Linz, on the Danube, houses a black basaltic statue of Isis to which pious worshipers pay their devotions, believing it to be an image of the Virgin Mary.

The halo of Egyptian Isis—the sun-ray crown—settled on Alexandrian Apollo and was later bestowed on both Christian and Buddhist saints. In late Assyrian representations of the seventh century B.C. the sun god Shamash wears a halo about the upper part of the body, and a Grecian vase of about 600 B.C. depicts Helios with an overhead disc. Later he is represented with spiked rays of light emanating from his head, and after 304 B.C. he regularly wears this spiked halo. The *Catholic Encyclopedia* contains biographies of more than one St. Isidore ("Gift of Isis"), most of them Spanish.

Twentieth-century Christmas celebrations in Rumania perpetuate the rites of Isis, or Dionysus: Lady Mary, adorned with the black robes of a nun, wanders through the world searching for her son. At the waters of the Jordan she addresses St. John:

"Listen John,
St. John!
Hast thou seen
Or hast thou heard
Of my Son,
The Lord of Heaven
And of earth?"

St. John assures her that he has heard of the crucifixion. He advises her to go to the fountain of Pilat;
there she will see her Son. Thither Mary goes, sobbing
and weeping. There she sees her Son, "like a luminous
Morning Star." She says to him:

> "O thou flower of basilic
> Why hast Thou allowed Thyself
> To fall into the hands of strangers,
> In the land of the heathen?"

"Jesus" explains that he has done so for the sake
of the world. He says:

> "The fields will be seen
> Green with grass,
> And the fountains with cold water,
> And whoever dies
> Will belong to God."

In this drama "Mary," it seems, personifies the
ancient Mother Goddess searching for her beloved
Osiris (or Adonis, or Dionysus), whose death and
resurrection ensure the revival of dormant nature.

The priests of Isis used the tonsure, which Saint
Jerome denounced in the fourth century as a pagan
practice. But the custom spread among the Christian
priesthood; in the fifth century it was common in the
monastic orders, and it was finally officially recognized by the Church, probably in the seventh century.

There is a close verbal and conceptual similarity to
New Testament sentiment in the Egyptian epitaph: "I
gave bread to the hungry and clothes to the naked, and

ferried across in my own boat him who could not
traverse the water. I was a father to the orphan, a
husband to the widow, a shelter from the wind to them
that were cold. I am one that spake good and told good.
I earned my substance in righteousness." An isolated
analogy, however, does not necessarily imply historic
contacts. In allegedly pre-European days Aztecs
voiced the sentiment: "Clothe the naked, feed the
hungry, whatever privations it may cost thee, for
remember their flesh is like thine, and they are men
like thee." Also: "Bear injuries with humility; God
who sees will avenge you"; and, "He who looks too
curiously on a woman commits adultery with his
eyes"—each a New Testament sentiment, and if the
translation is approximately literal, very similar in
phraseology to the New Testament.

In ancient Egypt incense imparted life to the dead
and could resurrect them; hence it was divine. This
concept and related practices probably account for
the adoption of incense in Christian churches.

Power came from the sun disc and entered the hand.
In the text of the *Book of Gates* , on the alabaster coffin
of Seti I, the "Great Hand" grasps the chain to which
the Four Sons of Horus are fastened and puts fetters
around the Underworld serpents and around Apep, god
of Evil, everlasting enemy of Ra, the Sun god. In
Christianity also the hand symbolizes God. In medieval
paintings He is represented by a hand projecting from
the clouds, sometimes open, with rays of light issuing
from the finger tips. The life-giving rays, signifying
the power of God, bestow life and blessings.

In many instances a hand is represented in the act
of benediction, that is, with two fingers extended. The

Old Testament refers to the hand being raised toward
God in worship (I *Kings*, 19:18; *Job*, 31:27). In west
Asia raising the hand was symbolic of invoking the
deity in oath, prayer, or supplication. On an ancient
monument the god Sabazius is raising the right hand
to bless his worshipers and preserve them from evil;
and a worshiper raises the right hand in worship and
reverence. Assyrians designated certain prayers as
"the lifting of the hand." These words precede a
prayer of Nebuchadnezzar II to Marduk.

In several Eastern countries amulets in the form of
an outstretched hand were attached to royal scepters,
spears and other weapons, to confer power on the
user. Among the Arabs, figures and drawings of the
right hand of Lady Fatima, the "Weaver," were
powerful amulets. Fatima, daughter of Mohammed by
his first wife, Khadija, is called Al-Zahra, the "Bright
Blooming." (This is also a name of Venus.) The
designation Al-Batul, "Clean Maid," or "Virgin," is
applied to Fatima even after her motherhood. Mohammed considered her to be one of the four perfect
women, the other three being his wife Khadija; Asia,
the wife of Pharaoh; and the Virgin Mary. Mohammedan commentators say that the hand of Fatima represents the entire religion of Islam and its fundamental
duties.

"I will wash mine hands in innocence," says *Psalms*,
26:6. A Mohammedan must wash his hands before
prayer and before a meal. While reciting the priestly
benediction a pious Jew extends the fingers so that the
number three is apparent: thumb extended, index and
middle fingers held together and counted as one, ring
finger and little finger together. A man who cannot

hold the fingers in this manner binds them in position with the fringe of his prayer-shawl. In some Christian churches, the officiating priest or minister, when offering the benediction, shows the sign of three by bending down the little finger and the adjacent one, and extending his thumb, index and middle fingers.

In Jewish legend God said to Moses: ''Take Joshua, lay your hand on him and bestow your spirit upon him, so that the children of Israel may accept him to be their leader while you are still alive, and honor him.'' Moses then led Joshua to ''Eleazar, the high priest, and before all the people of Israel, and in their presence he laid his hand upon Joshua, and bestowed his spirit upon him.''

The Egyptian practice of contracting with *ka* priests to ensure that the latter would take regular supplies of food to the tomb or mortuary temple of the contracting party after death, possibly inspired the Christian Mass for souls. In Egypt the practice was widely adopted on the theory that a man could not rely on the piety of his relatives to care for his needs after death.

The ancient Egyptians claimed that king Wo' issued from the thighs of the Nine Gods. Dionysus was born from the thigh of Zeus, the Hindu Aurva came out of the thigh of his mother, and Nishada from the left thigh of a prince. An old French poem declares that St. Anne, mother of the Virgin Mary, was born from the thigh of her father Phaneul.

Until the fifth century, Christian churches followed the model of Egyptian temples. They were divided into three parts, each associated with a secret or esoteric doctrine, known only to the builders, who were initiated into the Mysteries. The Catechumen—or disciples and

penitents—would use the front part, the ante-temple;
lay members and the faithful used the Nave; the third
part—the Sanctuary of the Gods—could be entered only
by priests, and consisted of a semi-circular recess
with an arched roof, which could be reached only by
steps leading up to it from the main floor. This same
plan, with modifications, was used in the construction
of Christian churches, and especially in the early
cathedrals, and the Free Masons who built these
cathedrals traced their origin to a Phoenician who,
they said, had built Solomon's Temple on the plan of
a temple to the Sun God at Karnak. The Christian
spire and steeple, inspired by the Egyptian pyramid
and obelisk, were confirmed by Pope Gregory the
Great as fitting symbols in the "worship of the True
God."

The Coptic Church

The cultural background and environment of the
Christians of Egypt (the Copts) were in many respects
different from those of Christians elsewhere, and the
Coptic faith reflects many characteristics of ancient
Egyptian times. In the great hall of the temple at
Heliopolis, in ancient Egypt, was an aged sycamore fig
tree, on whose leaves Thoth and the goddess Sefchet—
"the Lady of Writing," "the Ruler of Books"—wrote
the name of the pharaoh; the god Atum, following the
example of Sefchet, "wrote the name on the noble tree
with the writing of his own fingers." At Matarieh,
near Heliopolis, there is today a sycamore fig tree,
the "tree of the Virgin," at which, tradition states,
Joseph and Mary halted when in flight, with the Babe,

into Egypt, and there is good reason to believe that this Christian tradition is a modification of the ancient Egyptian belief regarding Thoth and Sefchet.

Mr. E. A. Wallis Budge (*George of Lydda*, London, 1930) thinks that the ostrich was worshiped, or reverenced, in predynastic Egypt. There are broken ostrich egg shells in predynastic tombs and in late Paleolithic, or Transitional burials in Berber North Africa. At the present day ostrich eggs are suspended in many Egyptian and Syrian churches and mosques, presumably a relic of this ancient practice.

In Coptic martyrdoms fearful monsters lie in wait to seize a dying man's soul. Each of these monsters has a prototype in ancient Egyptian funerary papyri. The god Horus slaying the demon Seth-Typhon became St. George slaying the dragon. An Egyptian bas-relief depicts the sparrow-headed god, equipped as a mounted warrior, thrusting a spear into the neck of a crocodile, emblem and incarnation of his demonic foe. A surviving rude Coptic relief of St. George and the Dragon is so thoroughly Egyptian in character and execution that it could easily be mistaken for a representation of Horus and Seth-Typhon. The equilateral triangle over the haloed head of this Christian hero—a symbol of the Trinity—appears on many Egyptian monuments. In the background is the bull Apis with what appears to be a decrescent moon over its back. Horus personified the vivifying and fertilizing forces of the physical world, the triumph of life over death and of good over evil. His feast, a vernal festival, was celebrated on April 23, now the anniversary of St. George. Tradition has it that this Christianized Egyptian god was born in Lydda, Asia Minor, that the Crusaders from the west

made his acquaintance there and took him back to
Europe, emblazoned on their banners. It might also
be noted that many Coptic monks were called "Har,"
a word believed to be derived from the Egyptian word
for Horus.

Ancient Egyptian traditions about the genitalia of
Set were introduced into some Christian apocryphal
works. In the Coptic book of the *Mysteries of Heaven
and Earth* Set is said to be 1700 cubits of the angels
in height, his mouth 40 cubits, his hand 70 cubits, his
feet 7000 cubits, and his phallus 100 cubits.

The ancient Egyptians celebrated twelve monthly
festivals. The Copts celebrated similar monthly festivals, under the Christian names of the Virgin, St.
Michael the Angel, and others.

Four gods lived in the Egyptian primeval ocean. One
of these gods presided over the birth of kings and
queens, and also assisted Osiris to rise from the
dead. An ancient Egyptian bronze relic in the British
Museum shows a frog mounting the end of a phallus.
We find that among Egyptian Christians the frog is
employed as a symbol of the Resurrection and is often
sculpted, along with the Coptic cross, on monuments
in the catacombs at Alexandria.

In an ancient Coptic relief of the Virgin and Child—
an exact imitation of the traditional Egyptian representation of Isis suckling the infant Horus—the necklace
of the Madonna is identical with that worn by goddesses
depicted on Egyptian monuments, which necklace was
also worn by ladies of royal rank during the period of
the pharaohs. The chair on which the Virgin sits—its
back shaped like the Egyptian hieroglyph for the letter
S—is an exact replica of the chair on which Egyptian

deities were enthroned and sovereigns sat in state.
The stiff and angular infant is fashioned precisely
like Horus, in typical Egyptian style. Nearby stands
Joseph, in rigid drapery, holding in his right hand a
tree and an instrument resembling a chisel, probably
to suggest carpentry. An Egyptian ideogram above
their heads symbolizes the sky, or the heavens, which
suggests their abode or their heavenly nature. A female
falcon with outspread wings, hovering over the group,
is the symbol of the solar god, who presides over
births and ensures an easy delivery.

In Coptic art Jesus is depicted as ascending to
heaven in the chariot of the sun god, the four steeds
of Helios being represented as the respective animals
associated with the Evangelists.

The beetle, for the ancient Egyptians, represented
the resurrection; the Christian Fathers used the beetle
as a symbol of Christ.

The tears of the Egyptian gods Shu and Tefnut fell
to the ground and became incense-bearing plants. The
Copts used the oil pressed from these plants as an
ointment in ceremonies of consecration.

The Copts chose their Patriarch by lot—a common
device among the Egyptians. The Superior of the convent of St. Anthony, in the eastern desert of Egypt,
names eight or nine monks whom he considers qualified
for this highest office in the church. Each name is
written on a separate slip of paper. These are then
rolled into a small ball and are put in a drawer. A
priest, with averted face, selects one of them and the
one whose name it bears is designated the Patriarch.
(Formerly the drawing was done by a young child—
as was the case, for example, as recently as 1959—

the child supposedly being directed in his choice by
the hand of Providence.)

When saying their prayers the Copts use a string of
forty-one beads, the number of the Egyptian assessor
gods. The five days following the 360-day period of the
ancient Egyptians were not reckoned as part of the
secular year, and were considered to be unlucky. These
same days are also unlucky days among the Copts.

In ancient Egypt a Nile festival associated with the
cult of Osiris was celebrated on January 6. On that
same day the Copts celebrate the festival of the
Immersion; they bless the river, pour holy water into
it, and people plunge into the stream.

Living amongst one another, the Copts and Mohammedans have mutually influenced each other. Among
the Jews in Cairo, under Mohammedan rule, wearing
the turban was compulsory. And there is Mohammedan
influence in the ritual of the Coptic prayers, which
are offered seven times a day at specified hours,
including sunset and midnight. The Copts also follow
the Mohammedan custom of removing their shoes
before entering a church, as well as wearing the
turban. On entering the church, the Coptic worshiper
goes to the door of the *heykel* (chancel), prostrates
himself, or makes a bow and a salutation with his
hand, before one or more of the pictures of the saints.
Sometimes he kisses the hand of one or more of the
officiating priests in the compartment immediately in
front of the *heykel*.

The Copts practise circumcision—an old Egyptian
custom—which they may have adopted from the Jews
or from Egyptian Mohammedans. Almost universally
they abstain from swine's flesh, as do Mohammedans,

although they eat the flesh of the wild boar. They also
abstain from the flesh of strangled animals, and do not
use the blood, which practice they justify on the basis
of *Acts*, 25:20,29.

The ancient Egyptians used bells as decorative
amulets. In *Exodus* (28:33) we are told of bells attached
to the vestments of Aaron, the high priest; their tinkling drove away evil spirits. *Isaiah* (3:16) suggests that
women attached bells to their skirts, "making a tinkling
with the feet," presumably for protection against evil
spirits. The early Copts used bells to drive away evil
spirits during the celebration of the Eucharist. In many
caravans today bells are tied to the necks of horses,
asses and camels, to keep away evil spirits.

An old amuletic sign, known as the *ankh* , or *anh* ☥,
was used by the dynastic Egyptians to indicate "life,"
"living," "everlasting life," "life which cannot die."
Each god, goddess, and divine being possesses it; it
maintains their life. They bestow it on kings and on
the souls of those acquitted in the Hall of Judgment.
Its recipients will live "one hundred thousand millions
of years." Those Egyptians who embraced Christianity
in the first century put this sign on their funerary
monuments alongside the Christian cross. In becoming
Christians, it seems, they did not stop being Egyptians.

CHAPTER TWO

Ancient Cultural Influences

Babylonian–Assyrian Influences

JAPANESE Buddhists say that a door which opens outward should not face northeasterly; from that direction come evil spirits and misfortune. The reference in *Psalms* (48:2) to the "sides" (or the "corner," or "uttermost") of the North, has been attributed to Babylonian influence. In the Babylonian concept, and also commonly among early Semites, the gods dwelt in the North. Mount Hermon, in northern Palestine, was sacred, as was Olympus to the Greeks, it being to the north of them. The *Talmud* states that God left unfinished the northernmost portion of the earth, saying: "Whoever professes to be equal to God, let him come and complete this corner which I have left unfinished, and thus all will know that he is equal to God."

"Northern" is a designation for Evil Impulse. In Christianity, after the pagan gods became Christian devils, the significance of the points of the compass was reversed. The South—the region of sunshine, warmth and light—became the abode of God and His saints, and North was the realm of demons. Consequently, in the celebration of the Eucharist the Epistle is read on the north side, as a proclamation to those who are in darkness. In Norman churches Christian emblems are on the tympana over the south door, and the emblems of demons are over the north door. Also, one should not bury on the north side of the churchyard.

The North Door in the end of the nave in the baptistry of Westminster Abbey, too small for a human body to pass through, was built to provide escape for the evil spirit exorcised by the water of the font. Early Christian churches faced northeast, with the choir in the southwest portion of the structure. This orientation has been attributed to the fact that early churches were erected on sites of demolished Roman temples, that they were usually built of stone and marble from the remains of the temples, and that the doorways of the latter faced east. In the third century this orientation was reversed, and has so remained.

Babylonia and Assyria probably are responsible for the fact that in Christian art and architecture the North is the region of meteorologic devils. Under the dominion and leadership of the "Prince of the Power of the Air" they produce storms and other convulsions in nature, and foster in man unruly passions and violent deeds. In *Isaiah* (14) Lucifer is depicted as saying: "I will sit upon the mount of the congregation high in the north." The evil principle, embodied in unclean beasts and exhibited in obscene and lascivious actions, is portrayed in sculpture and painting on the north side of the church, "the black side," dominated by Satan and his satellites. The south side, which shared the sacred character of East, is consecrated to saints, martyrs, famous theologians, and sturdy defenders of the faith. On its walls and windows are depicted the

triumphs of Christianity, the millennial reign of
Christ, the worship of the Lamb, and other appropriate
themes.

The *Talmud* rejects the view of the "heretics,"
that is, of the Essenes and the heathen, that the manifestations of God are in the East, and assigns them to
the West. But the early Church Fathers adopted a solar
theory, and the West became the sea of darkness and
the abode of demons. Hence the rose window was
placed high in the west wall of the church so that the
light of the Gospel might be visible to "those sitting
in darkness"; thus it "turneth the shadow of death
into the morning." Bells in towers at the west end of
the edifice terrify and discomfit demons and summon
the nations to Christ. In the earliest surviving churches
Christ is seated over the west entrance, to receive
the nations. After the twelfth century, when common
fears of the near advent of the Last Judgment had
passed, or were at least much mitigated, the space
above the door is usually occupied by an image of the
saint to whom the church is dedicated. Within the
churchyard a plot north of the edifice was set aside
for the bodies of criminals, children, and those who
died outside the pale of the Church. Thus the north
side could hardly be considered hallowed ground, an
opinion which persists today in some localities in
England.

In the Kristdala Parish of Småland, Sweden, the
graves extend east and west, with the head of the
corpse pointing eastward. The eastern part of the
cemetery itself is considered the most desirable. The
northern portion is reserved for suicides; formerly
their coffins were lifted over the north wall, but now

they are carried in through a small gate. Perhaps the concept of the North as the residence of evil spirits explains why people in southern Sweden believed that those in the North had great magic powers, and why the people of middle and southern Finland ascribed great skill in witchcraft to their neighbors of the North. In northwest Europe the terms *Lapp*, *Finn*, or *Lapp-Finn* became practically synonymous with sorcerer.

The Virgin of the Seven Swords, which seems a rather inappropriate Christian designation, presumably is the result of the adoption and adaptation of the Babylonian-Assyrian war goddess Ishtar, who is represented on ancient monuments with seven darts in her shoulders, their shafts forming a halo about her head. Representations of Ishtar, which Italian merchants brought to Europe, were interpreted as referring to the prophecy of Simeon that a sword should pierce the Virgin's soul. In the fifteenth century the motif was slightly modified to fit the Gospel record and received a permanent place in Christian art. (Representations of the Virgin in remote regions of the Middle East were said to be the result of the mission of the apostle Thomas.)

The use of aromatic incense was practiced in both Sumerian and Egyptian temples. The early Egyptians were acquainted with frankincense, and Herodotus states that in his time the Babylonians made similar use of it.

In a Hittite religious feast the main part of the ceremony suggests a meal. A table is brought into the room and is placed before the king; to a musical accompaniment the king breaks bread and drinks to the gods, or, literally, "the king drinks the gods."

Hand-washing terminates this ceremonial meal. In a Babylonian ceremony of offerings to a god, sometimes food and drink are presented to an image of the god, in a solemn swinging or up-and-down motion. The actual consumption of the food and drink was a mystery, and took place behind a linen curtain hung about the image and the sacrificial table, hidden from human eyes. The custom in the Eastern Church of surrounding the altar with linen curtains during the ceremony of transubstantiation is a continuation of this ancient rite.

Jewish Influences

Christianity originated as a sect of Judaism. Its founders were Jews; the first church was in Jerusalem, and its members were Jews. The messianic character of Jesus was supported by the claim that Joseph was directly descended from David and that Jesus, a Jew of the Jews, was the Anointed of the God of the Jews. He was crucified as King of the Jews; the intended mockery gives point to the allegation. He had gone to Jerusalem to participate in one of the most sacred annual rites of the Jews. He did not renounce Judaism; he stated that he came not to destroy but to fulfil the faith of the Prophets of Israel. He denounced mere following of the letter of the law, and endeavored to restore the spirit of the law and to instill new life into the old Jewish formulas.

Gibbon, who in most quarters was respected for his emphasis on truth, objectivity and sincerity, remarks: "The history of the church of Jerusalem affords a lively proof ... of the deep impression which the Jewish religion had made on the minds of its sectaries.

The first fifteen bishops of Jerusalem were all circumcised Jews; and the congregation over which they presided united the law of Moses with the doctrine of Christ. It was natural that the primitive tradition of the church which was founded only forty days after the death of Christ, and was governed almost as many years under the immediate inspection of his apostles, should be received as the standard of orthodoxy. The distant churches very frequently appealed to the authority of their venerable Parent, and relieved her distresses by a liberal contribution of alms. But when numerous and opulent societies were established in the great cities of the empire, in Antioch, Alexandria, Ephesus, Corinth, and Rome, the reverence which Jerusalem had inspired to all the Christian colonies insensibly diminished." (*Decline and Fall of the Roman Empire.*)

Rudolf Bultmann reminds us that Jesus, a Jew of the Jews, used in his teaching and preaching maxims and imagery of the Jews, even when criticizing certain Jewish practices, and that in declaiming against a too rigid legalism he was reverting to the denunciations of the Prophets of the Old Testament.

The pilgrimage, which became and remained significant in Christianity, as well as in Mohammedanism and Buddhism, was important among the Jews two thousand years ago. St. Paul continued the custom of making a pilgrimage to the Temple in Jerusalem. The custom probably persisted among the Christians until the destruction of Jerusalem by the Romans in A.D.70. From the beginning of the third century, or earlier, Christians made a pilgrimage to the Cenacle, the site of the destroyed Temple, and pilgrimages to the Holy

Land continued through the centuries which followed.
The Turks' interference with such pilgrimages was
one of the causes of the Crusades. After medieval
times the pilgrimage to Rome became a common
practice, and soon there were pilgrimages to many
places made holy by reason of association with a
saint, or because it was the site of a miracle.[1]

For a while the first disciples visited the Temple
(*Acts*, 3:1). Paul himself preached regularly in the
synagogue. The teachings of Jesus were consonant
with those of contemporary rabbis; in Talmudic
treatises of the period one can find comparable
passages, many of them expressed in almost identical
language, including the Sermon on the Mount. The
melodies of Gregorian chants echo those which can be
heard today in Jewish synagogues, perpetuating ancient
musical themes and cadences. The methods of indi-
cating vocalization or accent used in the Hebrew
Bible are similar to those later employed in the
musical notation adopted in Christian churches.

It is difficult to attribute to historical accident the
traditions (1) that Jesus—like Moses in an improvised
crib and Theseus in a chest—was laid in a manger,
(2) that he was watched over by friendly beasts—as
was Romulus by a wolf and Cyrus by a hound, (3) that
he was later reared—as were Romulus, Cyrus and
Oedipus—by a man of humble birth, (4) that he was
hidden in Egypt—as was Moses—from those who would
take his life, and (5) that he would return—as did many
another hero—to claim his kingdom.

[1] See ''Going on Pilgrimage'' in Ronald Knox, *Literary
Distractions* (New York, 1958), 11-35.

Human sacrifice, particularly the use of a victim dressed in royal robes, was widely spread in eastern Mediterranean lands. The Barabbas crucified with Jesus is reminiscent of the *Bar Abbas*, that is, Son of the Father, whom the Jews offered up as a vicarious sacrifice. Philo Judaeus, about 40 A.D., describes a mob at Alexandria which dressed up an old man, placed a sham crown on his head, a scepter in his hand, a purple robe on his body, and hailed him as Karabbas (presumably Barabbas).

It is long since forgotten that Christianity originated as a Jewish sect. Not until after its establishment did it occur to members of the new faith that the appeal was for Gentile as well as for Jew. This view was bitterly contested by some early Jewish Christians, notably by Peter, who later became the Rock of the Roman Catholic Church. Only after failure to convert a sufficient number of Jews, and a divinely inspired vision, was Peter convinced that Gentiles should be admitted to the faith. Not until Christianity was well embarked on its career did members of the cult attempt to break away from Judaism, and only after several generations were Judaeo-Christians regarded as a distinct element in the Church. The sacred book of the Jews—the Old Testament—makes up the major part of the sacred book of the Christians, and many Christian denominations, notably the Church of the Latter Day Saints, have been profoundly inspired by it.

Down to the present day, Judaism, especially through its theologians, has influenced Christian doctrines, particularly in Reform movements. Greeks, Romans and Jews gave thanks at meals, and Jews also gave thanks after eating. The Christian practice of

saying grace at meal time is a continuation of the
Jewish custom. The founder of Christianity was born,
lived, thought and taught as a Jew. The Disciples and
the Apostles were Jews. The earliest Christian
saints—Matthew, Mark, Luke, John, Peter, Paul—were
Jews. The first Christian church was in Jerusalem,
and its members were Jews. The God of Old Testament times and of the present day is the God of Jews
and of Christians.

Those who have most in common are often the least
likely to recognize it. What is common they submerge
under what is different and forget the indebtedness.
This is not peculiar to Christianity; it applies to sects
within Mohammedanism, Buddhism, Hinduism, Shinto,
as well as to a multitude of non-religious institutions.
A fiction that favors a faction is eagerly embraced
as support.

Iranian Influences

There is close similarity between the thought and
the phrase in *Luke* (16:19) and the declaration in the
Zoroastrian *Bahman Yast* (2:12): "Thus spoke Zara-
tust: O Auharmazd, righteous creator, I have seen a
celebrity with much wealth, whose soul, infamous in
the body, was hungry and jaundiced and in hell ... and
I saw a beggar with no wealth and helpless, and his
soul was thriving in paradise." Compare also with a
New Testament sentiment (*Mark*, 13:12, *Micah*, 7:6)
the Iranian description (*Yast*, 2:30) of latter days
when "all men will become deceivers, great friends
will become of different parties, and respect, affection
[hope?], and regard for the soul will depart from the

world; the affection of the father will depart from the
son; and that of the brother from his brother; the
son-in-law will become a beggar from his father-in-
law, and the mother will be parted and estranged from
the daughter." An ancient Iranian *Pehlevi* text contains the maxim: "When you want to sit down on a
seat at a wedding banquet, do not choose a seat high
up, lest they pull you away from that seat and put you
on a seat further down." This sounds very much like
Luke (14: 7-11). Possibly both writers are indebted to
the Aramaic original.

The account of Jesus' forty days of temptation in the
desert, when Satan took him to a high mountain and
offered him the whole earth, suggests the Iranian
ceremony designed to give control over demons to
him who fasts. The Iranian faster, alone in the desert
for forty days, is visited with apparitions of a lion and
other beasts. A devotee who remains steadfast until
the fortieth day attains mastery over encompassing
evil spirits.

The crucifixion of Jesus with two criminals suggests
the Iranian custom of crucifying a pretender or usurper
on three crosses, and of employing three victims for
a human expiatory sacrifice. The phrase in *Revelation*
(16:13), "three unclean spirits like frogs," recalls
the Iranian hatred for these creatures as minions of
Ahriman, that is, Satan, for they bring plagues and
death to men. The search of the Magi for the newborn
Christ-child implies Iranian influence, and the fact
that they were three was probably not accidental. The
Wise Men came from the East, following a star. In
Eastern belief, a star was placed in the sky when a
hero was born. Isidore tells us that the Magi, who

according to the Gospels announced the birth of Christ, were interpreters of the stars who were later known as *mathematici*, a term which in the ancient context of Isidore's time means both "mathematicians" and "astrologers." With them the Magi bring Persian gifts—myrrh, frankincense, and sweet-smelling herbs ever pleasing to Persian gods. And the apochryphal *Life of Jesus* states: "Now when the days were past, Magi came from the East to Jerusalem as Zerdoslot [Zoroaster] had predicted, bringing large gifts." Thus at an early date a Persian source of the Magi was assigned to the Nativity. It may also be noted that milk, which was used in Parsi ritual meals, was drunk ritually at the early Christian Eucharist, that Christian eschatology is an almost complete repetition of fundamental themes in Iranian eschatology, and that the dualism of the New Testament—scarcely present in the Old—is suggestive of Iranian influence.

Mithraism

Mithraism is indebted to *Genesis* for the account that when Mithra, before the creation of man, emerged from the solid dome of the sky, he was naked, hid in a fig tree, ate its fruit, and with its leaves made a garment for himself. He then went forth on his marvellous career to war against the forces of darkness, as Adam departed the Garden of Eden to encounter the hazards and hardships of human life. Mithra and his associates ended their earthly careers with a last supper, and his disciples commemorated his triumph in similar fashion.

When Mithra killed the bull, vegetation sprang from the carcass, wheat from the spinal cord, and a wine-bearing vine from the blood. Hence in holy feasts wine represented the blood of the heart. In Christianity, the fruit of the vine used at the Lord's Supper represents the blood of the crucified Christ, a practice for which the New Testament gives no warrant.

In the latter half of the second century A.D., according to Lucian, Mithraic practices included digging a pit, offering a sheep, and pouring its blood over the pit. The "God child"—Mithra—was adored at birth by shepherds who brought him gifts. He was called "The Good Shepherd," a messianic designation used in ancient Egypt by Ipuwer.

The head of the Mithraic faith, Pater Patruum, Father of Fathers, resided in Rome. The Christian designation of the Pope as Papa, Father, is possibly a borrowing from Mithraism. Adoption of Rome as the seat of the Pope may have non-Mithraic origins. The Pope's crown, or tiara, is a Persian (possibly also Mithraic) headdress. The pontifical throne which, according to tradition, was used by St. Peter, contains pagan carvings probably taken from Mithraism. It is of pagan, perhaps Mithraic, origin.

Mithra, born out of a rock—"the god out of the rock"—suggests the Gospel account that Jesus was born in a cave; and the words of St. Peter: "They drank of that spiritual rock ... and that rock was Christ," point up the same similarity. Mithra, like Moses, struck a rock, and from it came water of which his followers eagerly drank. He was called "The Rock." And Jesus said to Peter (whose name, in Greek, means *Rock*): "Upon this rock I will build my Church."

There are Mithraic remains on the Vatican Hill,
where now a great edifice symbolizes the Christian
"Rock,"—that is, Peter. Mithra embodied the seven
spirits of God; in *Revelation* the slain Lamb has
seven horns and seven eyes "which are the seven
spirits of God." In Mithraic baptism the priest made
a sign on the forehead of the baptized person, which
is presumably the origin of the similar early Christian
rite. (Tertullian tells us that the Devil is responsible
for this coincidence.)

The designation of Mithraic worshipers as "soldiers
of Mithra" is probably the origin of the designation of
Christians as "soldiers of Christ." The same meta-
phor is modified to fit present needs. In 1957 the
Reverend Billy Graham, evangelist, described his
recently completed "campaign" in New York City as
being like an "exploded bomb." After the artillery
shelling, he observed, "the local churches can move
in as infantrymen."

The exhortation that the followers of Christ "put on
the armor of light" (*Romans*, 13:12; see also *Ephe-
sians*, 6:11, 13) is, it seems, a transfer to Christianity
of the concept of Mithra as God of Light. Ascension
into the sky has its counterpart in the Elijah legend,
and the same motif occurs elsewhere in Mediterranean
cultures. Adonis, worshiped widely in the first century
of Christianity, was resurrected and ascended into the
sky in the presence of his worshipers. Other gods who
ascended into heaven were Dionysos, Herakles, Hyacinth, Krishna, and Mithra.

The Hindus worship an ammonite (fossil) found in
the Gandak River, which, they say, is Vishnu's form
as a golden bee. The god, when wandering in this shape,

attracted such hosts of bees that he assumed the form of a rock. The gods then made for each bee a dwelling in the rock. The bee, carved as a symbol of immortality on the early Christian catacomb tombs, is probably derived from pagan influences.

In ancient times honey, considered an antiseptic, was smeared on corpses to prevent putrefaction, and tradition has it that Alexander the Great was embalmed in this fashion. The practice is associated with the solar worship of Babylonians, Assyrians, and with the Mithra cult. Virgil tells us that the ancient Romans believed that bees are divine, they never die, and that they alone, among non-humans, ascend into heaven. The bee, in fact, personifies the soul.

In tenth-century Byzantium, bees were believed generally to be ill-tempered, and apt to attack anyone who approached their hive. They were especially antagonistic toward one who smelled of myrrh or of wine, and toward women, particularly those who were not virgins.

Bees were also considered to have great wisdom and political sense. They also liked music, were loyal to their "king," and could be bred from the carcass of an ox. The golden bull's head and the three hundred golden bees which were found in 1653 at Tournay in the tomb of the Merovingian King Childeric III, were inspired by the cult of Mithra. In France, in those early medieval times, the bee symbolized the sanctity of the sovereign; representations of bees decorated the mantle of the ruler in life and embellished his shroud in death.

Peter of Capua, among others, called Jesus the ethereal bee. Saints famous for good works were compared to bees: eloquent Church Fathers and other expounders of the faith—notably Chrysostom,Ambrose, Isidore of Spain and Bernard of Clairvaux—had "lips flowing with honey." In the hymns of medieval Mariolaters the queen bee of the hive is the favorite symbol for the Virgin Queen of Heaven.

Early Christians revered the ass. Jesus made his triumphal entry into Jerusalem on this beast which bears, in consequence, the outline of a cross in the black bar across the shoulders and the intersecting line above its backbone. The early Christians were probably also influenced by contemporary or older cults of the ass. Plutarch and Tacitus said that Jews adored the ass because it discovered springs of water in the desert during the flight from Egypt and the sojourn in the Sinai Peninsula. Perhaps the Christians applied this tradition to Jesus as the well-spring of eternal life. In any case, the importance of the ass among early Christians is abundantly proclaimed by Church Fathers and in early Christian art. All this prompted Tertullian to observe that some people imagined that the Christian God had the head of an ass. Enemies of the Gospel, he said, publicly exhibited a caricature of Christianity which showed a person in a long robe holding a book, but equipped with the ears and legs of an ass. Tertullian was indignant in his denial that such concepts were a matter of Christian belief.

Cecilius Felix wrote: "I hear that this basest of creatures [the ass] is worshiped by Christians, though I know not upon what insane persuasion." A rude drawing on the walls of an old Roman barracks or guardroom on the Palatine depicts a man kneeling before a crucifix on which is a human being with the head of an ass, and the legend: "Anaxomenos worshiping his God." Epiphanius declares that the Gnostics believed the Lord of Sabaoth had the head of an ass.

Greek and Hellenistic Influences

In ancient Greece the Twelve Gods held an exalted place in popular esteem, a concept which some associate with the twelve months (moons) and a central sun, and with the Christian idea of the twelve disciples. Some suppose that the deserter who betrayed the disciples symbolizes the intercalary month which was included at appropriate intervals in the calendar as a thirteenth month.

Although there is no evidence that such an association influenced New Testament writing, one is struck by the ancient Greek concept of the Twelve Gods, conceived in classical times as a sort of corporate body. To them a single altar was erected, and the oath "By the Twelve!" appears in Aristophanes. The Greeks conceived of "the Twelve" as a collective corporation, both in the classical period and later.

The "gates of Olympus" was a familiar figure of speech in Homeric Greek (e.g., *Iliad* , Book VIII) and suggests the gates of Heaven in the Christian tradition. Plutarch's account of Timoleon's voyage suggests the motif of the guiding star of Bethlehem: "And when he was now entered into the deep by night, and carried with a prosperous gale, the heaven seemed all of a sudden to break open, and a bright spreading flame to issue forth from it, and hover over the ship he was in; and, having formed itself into a torch, not unlike these that are used in the mysteries, it began to steer the same course, and run along in their company, guiding them by its lights to that quarter of Italy where they designed to go ashore." (*Lives*, Timoleon.)

Other Christian supernatural elements have an analogue in ancient Greece. It was said of Empedocles (died about 430 B.C.) that while guests were assembled with him and darkness had fallen, those present at this last supper heard a loud voice calling Empedocles, the heavens were illuminated, and he disappeared. An episode in Plutarch's *Lives* (Theseus) is reminiscent of an incident in the life of Jesus: "Lycomedes, either jealous of the glory of so great a man, or to gratify Menestheus, having led him up to the highest cliff of the island, on pretence of showing him from thence the lands that he desired, threw him headlong down from the rocks, and killed him."

In the Homeric Hymn, *To Hermes*, we read:

"Straight through the cave luck-bringing Hermes went and came to the rich inner chamber, walking softly, and making no noise as one might upon the floor.   ˋ

"Then glorious Hermes went hurriedly to his cradle, wrapping his swaddling clothes about his shoulders as though he were a feeble babe, and lay playing with the covering about his knees; but at his left hand he kept close his sweet lyre. But the god did not pass unseen by the goddess his mother."

Later, Hermes says:

"We will not be content to remain here, as you bid, alone of all the gods unfed with offerings and prayers. Better to live in fellowship with the deathless gods continually, rich, wealthy, and enjoying stores of grain, than to sit always in a gloomy cave; and, as regards honor, I, too, will enter upon the rite that Apollo has. If my father will not give it me, I will seek.''

The Greek cult of the cave in which the infant Hermes lived suggests motifs in the Bethlehem incident. Jerome, a Church Father, says the cult of the cave flourished in Bethlehem in his day.

Mad dogs were taken to a temple of Artemis at Rocca in Crete; there, those which were incurable threw themselves from a high promontory into the sea. This is reminiscent of the swine of Gadara who inherited the devils cast out by Jesus and rushed down the cliff to their own destruction.

In Babylonia the head of the community, or city-state, communicated with the god by going at night to the temple, sacrificing and praying there, then lying down and sleeping, so that the god might appear in a dream and give his instructions.

The practice of incubation which flourished in pagan temples was transferred to Christian churches, particularly in the Mediterranean region where the custom had flourished. At Epidaurus the gods' miraculous cures are recorded on marble slabs set up as permanent records. Here, to this day, at the festival of the Annunciation at Tenos, people gather from all parts of the Aegean. The sick and disabled sleep in the crypt of the church, as was done at ancient Epidaurus. Miraculous cures are reported. The practice of incubation was responsible for the reinterpretation in medieval times of the verse in *Matthew* (27:19) to the effect that the wife of Pilate, during the night preceding the trial of Jesus, had suffered on his behalf and had pleaded with Pilate to spare that just man. The word *suffer* was interpreted to mean that she had been ill and that Jesus, a twin, had appeared to her in a dream and had cured her. Pagan, and later, Christian twins were believed to appear to a dreamer and effect a cure or indicate a remedy.

Hellenism influenced Jewish thought in many ways. The influence is particularly evident in the apocryphal and pseudo-epigraphic Jewish literature in the period from the second century B.C. to the second century A.D. The literary language of the land in which Christianity originated was Hebrew; the language of Jesus and the disciples was the vernacular Aramaic; yet the New Testament was not written in Aramaic or in Hebrew but in Greek. This single fact attests to the importance of Hellenistic culture in the first and second centuries of Christianity.

The New Testament was written in so-called Basic Greek, at that time spoken from Marseilles in the western Mediterranean to Travancore in India. It was the most widely spread medium of communication for the learned world west of China. Those who share a language share its concepts, images and culture connotations. An example is the New Testament description of "the beginning." As *John* expounds it: "In the beginning was the Word, and the Word was with God, and the Word was God. The same was in the beginning with God. All things were made by him; and without him was not any thing made that was made. In him was life; and the life was the light of men." *Word* in the New Testament Greek is *Logos*. The context indicates that the New Testament writer's concept is the Stoic concept of *Logos*. It means "reason," "rationality," "in accord with a purpose." It is also

conceived of as "breath," or as "an air-like substance." It permeates the universe, gives it form, and
makes of it an entity. Anaxagoras taught that mind
transformed primeval chaos into orderly cosmos. St.
Thomas Aquinas (*Contra Gentes*) echoes the concept:
"The first mover and author of the universe is Mind,
and therefore its ultimate purpose is the goal of mind;
and this is Truth."

A language carries a penumbra of meanings and
nuances which evoke specific emotional and cultural
responses. Often, too, it carries concepts peculiar to
the language. Similarities between Stoic teaching and
Christian doctrine have been remarked upon from early
Christian centuries to the present. In the *City of God*
St. Augustine calls attention to the near-Christian
character of sentiments expressed by Roman Stoics,
notably Cicero and Seneca. If Marcus Aurelius had not
persecuted (or prosecuted) Christians, St. Augustine
might have included that Roman Emperor among the
near-Christians also.

Stoic teachings emphasize the importance of the
individual, the natural rights of man, the essential
sameness of men in all climes and social conditions,
and depict a world state in which all men are equal.
Contempt of circumstance and insistence that the individual can control his will are emphasized in Stoic
doctrine and in New Testament Christianity. Each
urges slaves to obey masters and exhorts masters to
be kind to slaves. The Stoics likewise taught that at
the end of a great cycle everything would be consumed
in a conflagration.

Concepts such as these were in the air which early
Christianity breathed. The concept of freedom in St.

Paul is almost identical with that of the Stoics. Paul's
notion that human life implies freedom does not occur
in the Old Testament. The wise man depicted by Stoics
is, like the wise man described by Paul, above external
necessity and the claims of society; like Epictetus he
proclaims power over earthly ills and fate itself. "All
things are lawful to me, but I will not be brought under
the power of any" (I *Corinthians*, 6:12) is his challenge.
The difference between the Stoics and Paul lies in the
source of their freedom. For the Stoics this is reason;
for Paul it is Christ—"I can do all things through
Christ who strengtheneth me" (*Philippians*, 4:13).[1]

The Christian's guardian angel is a close relative
of Socrates' *daemon*, the Roman's *genius*, and the
Stoic's inner holy spirit. Seneca says: "God is near
you, with you, within you.... A holy spirit sits within
us, watcher of our good and evil deeds, and guardian
over us. Even as we treat him, he treats us. No man
is good without God. Can any one rise superior to
fortune save with God's help?" In ancient Iran a good
and an evil daemon were responsible for one's good
thoughts and deeds and one's evil intentions and
actions respectively. The Cheremis of the Caucasus
has a guardian angel who sits on the right shoulder
and a devil who sits on the left. Everything one says
or does is recorded by the spirit to whose category it

[1] The influence of Stoicism on Christian thought has
persisted. In the seventeenth century Sir Thomas
Browne observed in his *Religio Medici* that "truly
there are pieces in the philosophy of Zeno and doctrine of the Stoics, which I perceive, delivered in a
pulpit, pass for current divinity."

belongs. When the person dies, the spirit with the longer list wins his soul. The Christian guardian angel is also suggested in the Parsi concept of the angel Sraosha, who has charge of the soul during life and aids it during its journey to the next world, especially during the first three days of that journey when the soul most needs such assistance.

The *Talmud* says: "Every man has three friends when Death summons him to appear before his Creator. His first friend, whom he loves most, namely his money, can not go with him a single step. His second, relations and neighbors, can accompany him only to the grave, and can not defend him before the Judge; while his third friend, whom he does not highly esteem—his good deeds—goes with him before the king and obtains his acquittal."

The Palaung of Burma believe that two guardian spirits sit on the shoulders of every living being, a good one on the left and an evil one on the right. Among the Siuai of Bougainville a man's ghost-familiar sometimes perches on his shoulder, and they converse in grunts and whistles. The Iban of Borneo have a constant invisible companion whose departure from a person brings on that person's death. The Chinese say that three goddesses of the corpse—nuns dressed in green, white and red, respectively—inhabit the body. On certain nights, determined by the almanac, a watch is kept lest these goddesses desert the body during sleep and go to heaven to inform the gods of one's sins.

Christianity began in the period and in the region of the Mystery religions, which placed much stress on initiation into the cult, all of which was undoubtedly familiar to early Christians. The drinking of the potion, *kukeon*, was important in Eleusinian ritual. This act of communion commemorated the sorrows of the goddess Demeter, whose daughter Persephone had been spirited away. "The great Queen Deo received it to observe the sacrament," is the explanation given us in the *Pseudo-Hesiod* (To Demeter, 211).

Orphic teachings were a potential inspiration for the Christian purgatory. To a place of darkness and gloom went the souls of those who had not been initiated and had not received the purifying rites. In this "hell"—actually a Purgatory—the soul contaminated by earthly things must suffer until the defiling elements have been burned out. It might then return to earth, be reborn, live again and have another opportunity to prepare for an eternal home in the Elysian Fields. Meanwhile, faithful friends among the living offered intercessory prayers and made sacrifices to mitigate the sufferings of the deceased.

Not every soul had an opportunity to obtain redemption. Certain of the condemned would receive no probation. As in Homer, many criminals remained eternally without hope in the darkness of Tartarus, where the wretched experiences which they endured in life were repeated and amplified. In the case of unjust decisions made on earth, appeal could be made in a "Court of Justice" in the Nether World and a hearing granted before judges whose wisdom permitted no error, and from whose decision there was no further appeal.

The mourning goddess Aphrodite, shedding tears over her slain lover, became in Christianity the Mater Dolorosa, weeping for her crucified son. When Paul preached in Syria and Cyprus the message of the

crucified and risen Christ, the essentials of that
doctrine were common knowledge among his hearers.
Many members of his gentile congregation were
familiar with the mystic drama depicting the death of
the god, and had participated in the rites of the cult
and experienced the religious satisfactions of which
Paul spoke. As for the interpretation of the death of
the Messiah as a sacrifice for the sins of the people,
this appears to have entered Christian doctrine through
Paul's writings. In the words attributed to Jesus, the
speech to Stephen, and the Epistle of James, there is
no intimation of such a concept. There may be a
historic connection between Paul's view on this subject
and the earlier Semitic concept of the death of the
man-God, which is also present in the Adonis cult. In
the first century A.D. this motif was familiar to
students of religion throughout the Roman Empire.

The influence of the Mystery cults on early Christian
practices is evident in the *photismos* (enlightenment),
which, by the time of Justin Martyr, was the designation for baptism. This designation was used in the
Greek Mysteries, as were the words *seal* and *sealed*,
applied to those who had passed the test. Some
initiates were literally sealed on the forehead—also a
Mithraic practice.

The term *mystery* was applied to baptism, and
other esoteric words current in the Greek Mysteries
were adopted by early Christian writers: words ex-
pressive of the rite or act of initiation, of the agent
or minister of it, and of the initiate or novice. These
designations have no prototypes in the New Testament.

Those admitted to the inner sights of the Mysteries
had a formula, or password, called *symbolon*, or

synthema; and the catechumens used a formula not
entrusted to them until the last days of their catechu-
menate, namely, the baptismal formula and the Lord's
Prayer. At other times the Lord's Prayer and the
creed were kept secret, as mysteries. To the present
day the technical term for a creed has been *symbolon*,
that is, "password."

Sometimes the baptized received the communion
after baptism; this was the case with devotees of the
Mystery religion who were initiated at Eleusis and,
after a day's fast, drank of the mystic *kukeon* and
ate of the sacred cakes. The initiated at Eleusis also
wore a mystic crown, as the Christian baptized were
sometimes crowned with a garland. This custom, which
was local, persisted at Alexandria until modern times,
with the divinities, surrounded by a blaze of light,
watching the initiation.

St. John Chrysostom, as though inspired by knowledge of this practice, depicts Christian baptism as
illuminated by the light of Easter Eve; and Cyril
describes the white-robed candidates for baptism
proceeding toward the church entrance, where darkness became the light of day. It was, indeed, only in

---

[1] The *kukeon* (*kykeon*) was, some scholars believe, a
mixture of an infusion of grain and cheese drunk in
commemoration of its having been offered to Demeter
while she wandered, distracted, in search of Persephone. The so-called *Homeric Hymn to Demeter* indicates that it was made of barley-groats and of water
flavored with pennyroyal. By partaking fully of the
appropriate ceremony one obtained the surety of a
life, or a fuller life, in the nether world.

the large and important churches that the rite of baptism was conducted, usually only once a year, at Easter Eve, sometimes at Pentecost. "See here is water, what doth hinder me to be baptized?" was a formula in this baptismal ritual, almost every item of which duplicated the ritual of the Mysteries.

As late as the ninth century in Rome the preparation for the annual baptismal ceremonies occupied the major portion of Lent. Candidates, after being examined and tested, fasted, and were then made cognizant of the secret symbols—namely, the Creed and the Lord's Prayer. On Easter Eve, shortly before noon, they assembled in the church of St. John Lateran. There the rites of exorcism and of renunciation—a feature of the ceremony today—were held. Pope and priests in sacred vestments, stood forth holding lights in front of them. These the Pope blessed. Lessons were read, psalms were sung, and there were other items characteristic of the Mysteries. Thus were the Mysteries transferred to the new religion, where they still thrive, as rites consecrated to God.

It is not known when, or by whom the sacraments of Baptism and Communion were instituted. Jesus was baptized, but did not baptize. At the Last Supper he compared the broken bread and the poured wine to his body and his blood, but there is no intimation in the New Testament that this was a sacrament in the sense that it is such in the Roman Catholic or the English Established Church.

In ancient Egypt the fish was a symbol of fertility, hence also of life. The custom of eating fish on Friday has been attributed to influence from the cults of the Mother-goddess, in many of which Friday was a sacred day of worship, and whose goddesses were patronesses of fishing. Perhaps these cults turned the attention of Christians to fish and led to the portrayal of it as symbolic of Christ, after the fact was noted that the Greek letters of the word *ichthus* (fish), give the rubric: Jesus Christ, the Son of God, the Saviour— *Iesous Christus Theou* [*H*]*uios Soter*.

The Manichaeans were aware that fish do not generate as do the beasts; hence it was safe to eat their flesh, though it was dangerous to eat the flesh of animals. This is one of the presumed origins of the Roman Catholic rule of fasting on Friday from other flesh, but allowing the eating of fish.

By the beginning of the second century B.C. the cult of Dionysos was known throughout the Graeco-Roman world. Livy states that at this time there were strenuous efforts to eject it from Italy. Jesus' riding of an ass into Jerusalem suggests the two asses associated with Dionysos, who had ridden them and later transformed them into a celestial constellation, perhaps the zodiacal sign of Cancer which, in the Babylonian zodiac, was the Ass and Foal. It indicated the zenith of the sun's power and the beginning of its decline toward winter. It may be that early followers of Jesus noted that his ministry culminated in his entry into Jerusalem and was followed by his descent into the tomb. He is described as riding, on this occasion (like Dionysos), on two asses, "an ass and a colt, the foal of an ass." A Gnostic gem displays an ass, a foal, the constellations Crab and Cancer, and an abbreviated Latin inscription, "Our Lord Jesus Christ, the Son of God." This is reminiscent of a drawing found on the Palatine, and now in the Collegio Romano Museum,

which depicts Jesus as hanging on the Cross, and
represents him as having the head of an ass. In Italian
folklore, Pope Benedict was strangled by the devil in
a forest, and after death he appeared in the likeness
of a bear with the head of an ass.

The ass is associated with the vine, the chief symbol
of Dionysos. Justin Martyr speaks of it as tied to a
vine. In *John* (15:1) Jesus is represented as saying, "I
am the true vine." In the *Teachings of the Apostles*,
the wine in the eucharist cup is referred to as "the
holy vine of David." The wine was, symbolically, the
blood of Jesus, and Jesus was, symbolically, wine, or
the vine. Some later saints used the concept rather
realistically. St. John of the Cross speaks of his soul
as "the inward wine cellar of my Beloved." St. Teresa
of Avila compares the center of the soul to a cellar,
"into which God admits us ... so as to intoxicate us
with the delicious wine of His grace."

Participants in the Dionysiac rites drank the blood
and ate the raw flesh of the sacred victim in which the
god was assumed to be incarnate. The animal which
embodied the god was sometimes a bull, a goat, or a
fawn—and possibly, before that, a human being. In
early Christian communities the sacramental (eucharist) bread was made into the form of a man: one
communicant ate the ear, another the eye, a third the
finger, and so on, in order of social rank. Pope Pela-
gius I forbade the continuance of this custom.

By at least the ninth century the practice of taking
Holy Water when entering the church was in vogue.
Previously, ordinary water in a large font outside the
church, or in the porch or vestibule, was used. In it
the communicant washed his right hand before entering

the church for Mass. Many fonts were inscribed with texts to remind the user of the importance of his being sure his soul was pure as a necessary condition of his taking part in the Mass. It was from this that the custom arose of bestowing a special blessing on the water, with all the sacramental imputations of grace which derived therefrom. The original purpose of washing the hand was to make it properly clean to receive the Host placed upon it. However, after the abandonment of the custom of receiving the Host upon the hand, the use of the water continued, the people blessing themselves with it.

Each year, in spring or early summer, a three-day festival was held in honor of Hyacinth, a Spartan god or hero who was accidentally killed by a blow. On the first day he was mourned as dead; on the second day his resurrection was celebrated with great rejoicing; on the third day his ascension, it appears, was commemorated. Sculptures at his tomb show him ascending to heaven accompanied by his virgin sister and by angels, or goddesses. St. Jerome (died 420) sadly observed: "My own Bethlehem ... was overshadowed by a grove of Tammuz, that is, of Adonis; and in the very cave where the infant Christ had uttered his earliest cry lamentation was made for the paramour of Venus." Attis (Adonis), the Good Shepherd, was the son of Cybele, the Great Mother, or of the Virgin Nana, who conceived him. In the prime of manhood he mutilated himself and bled to death at the foot of a pine tree, a tree sacred to him. In Rome the festival of his death and resurrection was held March 22–25. In Phrygia, Gaul, Italy, and other localities in which worship of Attis was prevalent, the Lord's Passion

was celebrated on March 25. On March 22 a pine tree
was felled and to its trunk was fastened an effigy of the
god, which was later buried in a tomb. Hence, perhaps,
the reference in *Acts* (5:30) to Jesus being "slain and
hanged on a tree." On March 24, the Day of Blood, the
High Priest, impersonating Attis, drew blood from his
arm and offered it in lieu of the blood of a human victim. This practice may have inspired the New Testament statement in *Hebrews* (5:11-12): "Christ being
come an High Priest...neither by the blood of goats
and calves, but by his own blood...obtained eternal
redemption for us." During the night of March 24, the
priests of Attis went to the tomb; it was illuminated
from within, and was empty. They learned that on the
third day the god had risen from the dead. On the
following day, with much rejoicing, they celebrated his
resurrection. A sacramental meal was eaten, initiates
were baptized with blood, their sins were washed away
and they were "born again."

These pagan ceremonies were conducted in a sanctuary on the Vatican Hill, where now stands the
Mother Church of St. Peter, under whose lofty structure have been found several inscriptions depicting
these ceremonies. Christianity has sanctified both the
place and the rite. March 25, regarded as the spring
equinox, was considered as the most appropriate day
to revive a god of vegetation who had been dead or
sleeping during the winter. Probably early Christian
ecclesiastical authorities assimilated the Easter
festival to the festival of the death and resurrection of
Adonis.

Easter rites still observed in Greece, Sicily and
south Italy bear striking similarities to the Adonis

rites. Possibly the Church consciously adapted the Easter festival to this heathen predecessor; if so, the adaptation likely occurred in Greek-speaking rather than in Latin-speaking lands; the worship of Adonis, which flourished among the Greeks, appears to have had little influence elsewhere in Europe. It was not accepted by official Roman religion. An Easter celebration still held in Sicily is an obvious continuation of the Adonis cult, in a locality where doubtless it once flourished. There the gardens of Adonis are still sown. Before Easter, women sow seeds in plates of water; and on Good Friday they place the sprouted plants on a sepulchre containing an effigy of the dead Christ. The grief-stricken people wail over the effigy and bury it. At midnight the bishop announces that Christ is risen and the audience shouts in jubilation; guns are fired, fireworks are exploded and in high revelry a feast is begun in which the wine flows freely. A recent student of the subject reports that this celebration is no more than a sensuous orgy devoted to the worship of Adonis, in the guise of a Christian celebration of the resurrection of Christ.[1]

Until recently scholars had supposed that Gnosticism was a cult which originated within Christianity; however, it is now known to have been one of many Near East influences which affected a portion of the new sect. Gnostics were organized in a community somewhat after the manner of those of the mystery cults, with their sacraments, baptisms, sacred meals, ascetic practices and ritual purification. A Gnostic

[1] Frank H. Marshall, in *The Religious Backgrounds of Early Christianity*, St. Louis, 1931.

hymn of thanksgiving (*Odes of Solomon*, 25) reveals
some of the aspirations of members of the sect:

> For thou didst stand by to champion my cause
>   Didst redeem me and succour me.
> Thou didst keep back mine adversaries
>   That they showed their faces no more.
> For thy Person was with me,
>   And it saved me in thy grace.
> I was despised and rejected of many
>   And was in their eyes as base metal.
>
> But I received strength and succour from thee.
> Thou didst set lights on my right and my left,
>   That there might be no darkness round about me.
> I was bedecked with the covering of thy Spirit
>   And stripped off the garments of hide
> For thy right hand hath exalted me,
>   Thou hast removed sickness from me.
>
> I became whole in thy truth
>   And holy in thy righteousness.
> All thine adversaries yielded before my face;
>   I became the Lord's in the name of the Lord.
> I was justified by his loving kindness,
>   And his peace endureth for ever and ever. Amen.

Italian, Graeco-Roman, and oriental cults used incense. Early Christians excluded it from their service.
For a long time, during periods of persecution, the
use of incense was a test in determining whether the

accused was a Christian. By the end of the fourth century, however, incense was being used in Christian churches in Jerusalem; in the sixth century, in Antioch, and by the fourteenth century, in Western Europe.

The present-day custom in the Greek Orthodox Church of throwing the hair cut from a child's head into the baptismal font when the child is baptized, and also when the hair is first cut, is a modification of a rite practiced in ancient Greece. After the fifteenth century the Western Church dropped this custom.

The excommunication authorized and practiced by the Church has a precedent, if not direct inspiration, in the banishment practiced in Greece and Rome. The formula of a Greek ban is recorded by Sophocles: "I ban him, whosoever he be, from this land whose royal power and scepter I wield. Let no one receive him or speak a word to him, nor give him part or lot in prayer and sacrifice to the gods, nor in the lustral water: but let every man thrust him from his doors, since he is to us a pollution [*miasma*]. So the oracle of the Pythian god has but now revealed to me."

The use of the church edifice as a sanctuary has an analogue in Greece. In Athens a suspected murderer might take sanctuary on the Areopagus. There, before his accusers and the Council of State, he might swear to, and plead, his innocence. If he was acquitted, the avenging kin of the murdered man must look elsewhere for a victim. Christian scholars of the early period were undoubtedly acquainted with these practices; that they inspired analogous customs in Christendom is not, however, demonstrable from documentary evidence.

There is precedent for Christian practice in the custom referred to by Hippocrates (460?-359? B.C.):

"We mark out the boundaries of the temples and the groves of the gods, so that no one may pass them unless he be pure, and when we enter them we are sprinkled with holy water, not as being polluted, but as laying aside any other pollution which we formerly had." (*On the Sacred Disease*)

Some Christian concepts and practices associated with All Souls' Day may be indebted to Olympian Dionysos. In a Greek ceremony in which the dead were appeased, the spirits of the dead were released by opening the wine jars, of the kind used as funeral jars and to hold seed. Each man invited to his house those spirits for which he was responsible, taking care also not to offend his neighbors. After the spirits had been properly feasted and propitiated, they were literally swept back to their former resting-place, and the streets and houses were cleansed of their contaminating presence. Some practices still in vogue among the folk of northern Europe suggest a continuation of this practice, or at least a similar motivation.

Early Roman and Other Italian Influences

Plutarch writes (*Lives*, Romulus): "To Tarchetius, they say, king of Alba, who was a most wicked and cruel man, there appeared in his own house a strange vision, a male figure that rose out of a hearth, and stayed there for many days. There was an oracle of Tethys in Tuscany which Tarchetius consulted and received an answer that a virgin should give herself to the apparition, and that a son should be born to her, highly renowned, eminent for valor, good fortune, and strength of body. Tarchetius told the prophecy to one

of his own daughters, and commanded her to do this
thing; which she avoiding as an indignity, sent her
housemaid.'' The same writer declares that Numa
Pompilius was admitted to ''celestial wedlock in the
love and converse of the goddess Egeria.''

That Plutarch was familiar with the concept of
impregnation of a virgin by a god—a belief widely
spread in Mediterranean cultures—is shown by his
reference to similar accounts. He speaks of ''those
very ancient fables which the Phrygians have received
and still recount of Attis, the Bithynians of Herodotus,
the Arcadians of Endymion, not to mention several
others, who were thought blessed and beloved of the
gods; nor does it seem strange if God, a lover, not of
horses or birds, but men, should not disdain to dwell
with the virtuous and converse with the wise and tem-
perate soul, though it be altogether hard, indeed, to
believe, that any god or daemon is capable of a sensual
or bodily love and passion for any human form or
beauty.'' And he mentions comparable Egyptian and
Greek concepts.

When (says Plutarch) Numa was appealing to the gods
as to whether he was acceptable as a king, ''the chief
of the augurs covered Numa's head, and turned his face
to the south, and, standing behind him, laid his right
hand on his head, and prayed, turning his eyes every
way, in expectation of some auspicious signal from the
gods.'' Perhaps this practice is historically associated
with the Christian rite of the laying on of hands.

In order to capture the attention of their audience,
Roman orators held out the hand, with the thumb and
first two fingers extended and the other fingers
pressed against the palm. This is the manner in which

a bishop gives a blessing. It is thus represented in Exeter Cathedral on the leaden coffin of Bishop Bitton who died in 1307.

The regalia of the Roman Catholic Church owes much to ancient Rome. The clerical gown—Roman toga—persists also in English courts of law and in American and European academic garb. The chasuble and alb correspond to the tunic and cloak worn by Jews, Greeks, and Romans. The Cardinal's crimson was inspired by the Roman Emperor's distinctive garment. By the end of the seventh century Roman civilian dress was stylized in ecclesiastical garments, as was the Roman official title of Pontiff, "Keeper of the Bridge," now a designation of the Pope.

At the festival of the Parilia on April 22 a Roman peasant wetted his hands with dew and turned to the east, as an Italian peasant today turns to the east and uses holy water when he prays for the safety and increase of his flocks.

The apotheosis of Emperors by the Roman Senate probably inspired the Christian practice of canonization of saints. Traditionally, apotheosis dates from the times of Romulus. A Senator of that day, Proculus Julius, publicly stated that he saw Romulus transported to the sky, where assuredly he had a place among the gods. In Jewish legend, when the soul of Moses was summoned, "God bent over the face of Moses and kissed him. At once the soul leaped up in joy and with the kiss of God flew into Paradise."

In ancient Egypt, favored persons were permitted to kiss the royal foot instead of the ground in front of the pharaoh. Kissing sacred objects, such as the foot of the statue of St. Peter in his Basilica in Rome, the ring of a Pope, Cardinal, or Bishop, or kissing the Bible when taking an oath, may be a transfer from the Greeks, Romans, or the ancient Arabs, all of whom practiced this method of adoring holy things. Cicero says that the mouth of a statue of Hercules at Agrigentum was worn away by the kisses of his devotees, and Lucretius speaks scornfully of similar manifestations of piety, which Christianity adopted, continues and honors today.

In St. Gil (Spanish Catalonia) on September 1, shepherds in full costume wearing sheepskin coats and carrying staves and crooks, attend Mass, together with their dogs and best rams. On September 29 on St. Michael's Day at Arudy there is a Procession of the Sheep. A sheep from the communal flock is decorated with ribbons, a huge bell is hung from it, and it is led to Mass. At the Elevation of the Host the sheep, substituting for the *enfant de choeur*, is made to ring the bell, and is later presented to the priest. The rite flourishes in Aragon and Catalonia, and in Provence almost to the Basses Alpes.

The custom of blessing domestic animals, common in Latin Europe and Latin America, may have originated in the ancient Roman practice in which the Vestal Virgins gave to assembled shepherds the ashes of unborn calves mingled with horse's blood, for the fumigation of flocks and herds. In tenth century Byzantium fumigation was a means of purification: flocks and herds, shepherds and herdsmen, were thus purified in a spring festival. In New York City in 1961 a Jesuit priest blessed the assembled pets of children.

The Sibylline Oracles were used by both Greek and Latin Church Fathers, and patristic writings contain some eight hundred lines of them. In Lactantius there are fifty-one quotations or allusions to these prophecies. The so-called "lots of apostles and prophets," the practice of opening the Bible at random and taking omens from the first passage that meets the eye, is almost certainly an inspiration from the old Virgilian lot—the *Sortes Vergilianae*—of classical antiquity.

A "snow miracle" witnessed by Pope Liberius on August 5, 352, led to the consecration of the Roman Basilica (later called Santa Maria Maggiore) and was celebrated in medieval times as the *Dedicatio B. M. V. ad Nives*. Actually it was a continuation of the Roman custom of strewing flowers at dedication festivals. It is, of course, a considerable exaggeration to say, as Santayana does (in Persons and Places) that the underlying basis of all this is a "Santa Maria Sopra Minerva," but there is much truth in the assertion.

The monstrant was introduced not earlier than the thirteenth century. In the fifteenth century it was common in all large churches. Its Latin designation is not presumptive evidence that it was a Roman, or an Italian, inspiration. The language of ancient Rome, however, became the language of the liturgy of the early Western Church and has remained so in the Roman Catholic Church throughout its domain. It was not until 1963 that permission was given to say the Mass in the language of the locality.

CHAPTER THREE

Saints

FOR a long time, beginning with Jews who wrote the
New Testament, pagan heroes have been successful candidates for sainthood. Unlike the Jews, many
of these pagans were not converts to Christianity, even
though Christianity has posthumously claimed them as
its own.

In Greece several classical gods now function as
Christian saints. Apollo became St. Elias; St. Deme-
trius plays the role of Demeter; St. Artemidoros
personifies Artemis; St. Eleveterius takes the place
of the goddess Eleutheria; St. Charalambus performs
functions which fell to Aesculapius; Pan became St.
Anarguris; St. Nicholas carries out the duties of
Poseidon. In Malta the Venus temple became the Church
of St. Venera—a local saint not in the official Christian
calendar. A Celtic goddess, comparable in that culture
to Venus in the Greek, became St. Bride (Bridget). The
Dioscuri, Castor and Pollux, the savior twins, became
Saints Cosmo and Damian (Kismas and Damian).
Dionysos, many of whose attributes were associated
with John the Baptist, became St. Denis of Paris.
Diana Illythis became St. Yllis of Dole; Dia Victoria
became St. Victoire in the Lower Alps; the Egyptian
god Horus, who speared and slew the monster which

typified or represented the evil deity Seth, became
(some believe) St. George.

Gibbon, who was not particularly fond of traditional
heroes, says (in his *Decline and Fall of the Roman
Empire*) that: "George,... surnamed the Cappadocian,
was born at Epiphania in Cilicia, in a fuller's shop....
From this obscure and servile origin he raised himself
by the talents of a parasite; and the patrons whom he
assiduously flattered procured for their worthless
dependent a lucrative commission, or contract, to
supply the army with bacon. His employment was
mean; he rendered it infamous. He accumulated wealth
by the basest arts of fraud and corruption; but his
malversations were so notorious, that George was
compelled to escape from the pursuits of justice."
And more of a similar nature.

Although his identity was not known, St. George was
worshiped in the Near East from the third century on.
About the tenth century, stories of his martyrdom were
virtually identical to the stories told about the death
of Adonis. In the sixteenth century the Christian com-
mentator Hospinian stated that "in allegory, St. George
stands for Christ, the Dragon is the Devil, and the
citizens of Silena are the human race redeemed by
Christ." A modern scholar believes that Hospinian's
interpretation persuaded the Church to elevate George
to sainthood, on the basis of an ancient fable sprung
from such pagan dragon stories as that of Perseus and
Andromeda.[1]

[1] See the discussion by E. R. Leach, "St. George and
the Dragon," in G. E. Daniel, ed., *Myth or Legend?*,
New York, 1956.

The feast of St. Agatha is celebrated three days after Christmas. As a result of confusion of her name with another *langue d'oc* word, in the Pyrenees she became Santa Gato (Saint Cat).

In England and the United States the cult of St. Christopher enjoyed a considerable boom during a tug-boat strike in the fall of 1938, when Commodore Robert, unaided except for the acknowledged assistance of St. Christopher, brought the ocean liner *Queen Mary* safely into dock in New York harbor. This supposedly impossible feat sent the English scurrying for St. Christopher charms, and the supply was soon exhausted. On this side of the water, farsighted merchants laid in a variety of St. Christopher medals, from door keys to pocket calendars and automobile tags, and a fashionable Fifth Avenue store devoted much newspaper space to advertising them. Before the end of the year a shrine of St. Christopher was installed in the Roman Catholic Church of St. Columba in New York City, as part of a ceremony establishing a St. Christopher's Guild. On St. Christopher's Day in 1941 the Rector and Assistant Rector of the church were kept busy from nine in the morning until evening, blessing automobiles and other vehicles, including bicycles, home-made scooters, and baby carriages. The Rector, Father Dunleavy, cautioned against the error of believing that a picture or medal of the saint was an automatic guarantee of safety, and a present-day Catholic author[1] warns his readers that the wearing of a religious medal means only that one has confidence

[1] Raymond W. Murray, in *Introductory Sociology*, New York, 1946.

in the power of a saint to intercede with God, and that it is a sin to use such objects in a superstitious way.

St. Michael (the Gael Neptune) is the patron of the sea, of boats, of horses and horsemen, and also the guardian of high places, from which he has ousted earlier local divinities or demons, of which latter there is abundant testimony in the many *St. Michael's Tors* and *Mounts*. As an archangel he watches over the souls of the dead, weighs them in the balance, and escorts the good ones to the abode of bliss. A few years ago, in some localities in Ireland, there were deposited with the corpse a piece of candle, a coin, wine, and spirits: the candle to give light to the deceased on his dark journey to the nether world; the coin to pay his fare over the river of death, and the "food" to sustain him during his passage.

Many Irish graves contain a short clay pipe, placed there, perhaps, for the use of the departed. In the West Highlands a wax candle, a gold coin, a hammer and a pair of scales were put in the grave with the body. With the hammer the soul will knock for admittance to the entrance to the next world. The scales will be used to weigh the soul, while St. Michael watches the beam so that the Devil can not, with "claw of hand or talon of foot," pull it down in his favor. Meanwhile, angels from heaven and demons from hell preside at their respective sides of the scale. This is an almost exact duplication of the Egyptian scene of the weighing of the soul before Osiris and the assessors (judges).

The festival of St. Michael, for which extensive preparations are made, is celebrated on September 29. On the preceding day—St. Michael's Eve—a male lamb, without blemish, is killed, struan-cakes are baked and carrots are gathered. In preparation for the circuiting on the following day it is a point of honor for every man to steal a neighbor's horse and ride away with it. On the day of the ceremony there are pilgrimages to the burial ground and circuiting, the lamb is cooked and its flesh and the struan-cakes are distributed. All except the very young and the very old, who remain at home to tend the flocks and grain, participate in the circuiting. After prayers in the church, the participants remount and continue the circuiting of the burial ground, approaching it from the east, and following the sun's course, in the name of the Trinity. The priest, riding a white horse and wearing a white robe, leads the procession, followed by the people in a column two to ten abreast. They proceed clockwise, singing the *Iolach Micheil*, the Song of Michael the Victorious. Each then presents a handful of carrots to his companion, and they exchange gifts. Athletic contests and dances follow. Symbolic dances include the "Carlin of the Mill-dust," in which a man and a woman are paired; the man carries a wand in his right hand, waving it over his head and that of the woman. He touches her with it and she falls down at his feet as though dead. He bemoans the death of his Carlin, dances and gesticulates around her body, raises her right hand, examines the palm, breathes on it and touches it with his wand.

In the seventeenth century, when the Spaniards were established in the Southwest United States, each pueblo had a church and a patron saint. One of the favorite Spanish saints is Santiago, whose powers are especially beneficent for horses. In the Southwest, Santiago, the Apache San Geronimo, and a similar Indian spirit with the name of Boshaiyanyi, are personified by men riding small hobby horses. They also ride through the corrals and sprinkle holy water on the horses.

There has been much amalgamation of Christian saint with aboriginal hero or mythic being. In Keresan pueblos, the Spanish Santa Ana and Santiago are the Indian spirits Masewi and Oyoyewi, or Spider Grandmother. John the Baptist is now mother of non-Indians, Naotsityi; Jesus is mother of Indians, Utctsityi. As the natives formerly offered prayersticks to Indian gods, so now they offer them to the Christian God. Three centuries of contact with, and adoption of, Catholicism or Protestantism has not driven out the aboriginal spirits or lessened their appeal.

The story is similar among the Maya of Yucatan, where Catholic saints merge with pagan deities. The roles once played by the guardians of the four cardinal points—the Maya Pauhtuns—now fall to the Archangel Gabriel or other Christian saints. The ancient rain-gods—the Chacs—are now led by the Archangel Michael. In British Honduras, also, the aboriginal gods are now embodied in the saints brought by the conqueror: the patron saint of rain is St. Vincent, and St. Joseph is the guiding spirit of the corn-field.

Christianity has indeed grafted on to itself a great many non-Christian elements of the most diverse character and origin. St. Augustine is indebted to both Plato and the Stoics; St. Thomas Aquinas expounds the philosophy of Aristotle. Monasteries, cathedrals and parish churches reflect a multitude of aspects of the history of the past; in many cases they embody elements once hostile to the Christian faith, giving good ground for the observation that Christian men guard even the things of the heathen.

CHAPTER FOUR

Hinduism and Buddhism

THE Hindu ceremony of purification suggests the Roman Catholic shriving. A dying Brahmin recites, "in spirit," that is, silently, if he is too weak to articulate distinctly, certain *mantrams*, or sacred formulas, which ensure deliverance from his sins. The Hindus regard human nature as corruptible and corrupted and therefore in need of purification, so that the soul may regain those attributes which it has lost through sinning. Somewhat as in the Christian Bible, the soul is sometimes conceived as the breath—as when God imparted life to a clay image by breathing into it.

The burning of candles at the bier, in Christianity, suggests the lighting of lamps at the Hindu *Divali* festival to avert premature or unnatural death. The god of death—Yamadharma—through his messenger, assured those who burned lamps for five days that they would escape from Asvinvad; those who burned them for thirteen days would escape premature and unnatural death. During the Divali festival lighted torches are carried through the streets, to the cry of *"dip dipalyo."* Villagers present the government officials with torches to give to their servants to carry. Cowherds make out of *kanchi* grass an image of a large-hooded cobra; they fold the hood to form a niche in it, place a light in the niche, and then carry it from house to house and wave it around the cattle, holding the torches aloft toward the sky in order to provide light by which those unfortunate souls that have fallen into hell might reach heaven.

Similarities between the founders of Christianity and Buddhism, as well as the many resemblances between the religions themselves, have long impressed and puzzled students of comparative religion. There is no record of transmission from one region to the other either before or during the early Christian period. However, as early as 2700 B.C. there were some culture contacts between the Indus Valley and Mesopotamia; pre-Christian influences from Iran reached the Mediterranean region, and Hellenism penetrated into India. And later, about the time the early Christians were beginning to formulate some of their doctrines, the cult of Mithra was brought from India to Rome.

It may be that elements of Buddhism were known in the Mediterranean environment of early Christianity. In the latter part of the sixteenth century Father Matthew Ricci, a Jesuit priest who had gone to China as a missionary, remarked on the similarities between the doctrines of the Buddhist sect of the Amida and the practices and doctrines of Christianity. The Buddhist doctrine of the transmigration of souls, he noted, recalled a somewhat confused form of the teachings of Pythagoras, with tenuous overtones of the Christian Gospels. Like Christianity, the Buddhists had a trinity of three gods in one. They also preached reward for the virtuous in heaven and punishment in hell for the wicked. They practiced celibacy to the extremes of rejecting marriage and abandoning their homes and families. Father Ricci also saw some resemblance between Buddhist and Christian ceremonies, such as a Buddhist chant similar to the Gregorian, the use of statues in their temples, and the wearing of vestments not unlike the capes of the Christian priest.

Among the elements common to both Buddhism and Christianity we may include: monasticism, tonsure, regalia, and vows remarkably like those of Western monasticism; the use of bells, incense, candles, and rosary; saints; prayers for the repose of the soul; the concept of hell-fire; and several institutional and ritualistic complexes or traits, such as, for example, the since discarded rule that Buddhist priests might not marry, or eat fish or meat.

Rawlinson[1] attributes the striking resemblances between Tibetan Lamaist rituals and those of Roman Catholics to the influence of the Christian Church in Persia. These resemblances, which suggest more than coincidence, startled the Abbé Huc when he visited Lhassa in 1842. "The crozier, the mitre, the chasuble, the cardinal's robe," he observed, "the double choir at the Divine Office, the chants, the exorcism, the censer with five chains, the blessing which the Lamas impart in extending the right hand over the heads of the faithful, the rosary, the celibacy of the clergy, their separation from the world, the worship of saints, the fasts, processions, litanies, holy water,—these

[1] H. G. Rawlinson, *Intercourse between India and the Western World*, Cambridge, 1916.

are the points of contact which the Buddhists have
with us!''

Similarities between many elements in both Christian and Buddhist doctrines were pointed out in 1819
by a Western visitor in his observations about "the
religion derived from the Bramins [Brahmans],
transplanted from India to Japan.'' He writes: "The
facts, connected with this religion, manifest in a most
extraordinary degree the rapid spreading of the knowledge, though corrupted, of the Christian religion to the
eastward of Judea. About the year A.D. 55, the Chinese
emperor, Mimti, heard of a sect in India called the sect
of Xaca, and he was so pleased with their tenets, as to
send special messengers thither, with orders to acquire a perfect knowledge of their forms and opinions.
About the year A. D. 62, these messengers, returning
by way of Japan, found the tenets of Xaca already
introduced there,—a brief sketch of which will suffice
to prove the fact in question. Some of these were that
there are future recompenses established for virtue,
and punishment for vice: that good men after death
are received into a place of happiness where all desires are fulfilled, but the wicked shut up in a place of
torment; that Xaca is the saviour of mankind; that he
was born of a female in order that he might recall
men to the way of salvation from whence he had previously seen that they had strayed; that he came to
expiate the sins of the world, in order that, after death,
they might acquire a happy resurrection; and that the
Godhead consists of three persons in unity—a coincidence in chronology and doctrine which strikes at the
very root of those assertions of infidelity, that would
look for the origin of the Christian gospel, in the

corrupted traditions of the East, supported by the
unfounded assertions of anterior antiquity.... The
subject is well worth the attention of Christian Divines,
anxious to overturn the strong hold of modern scep-
ticism.

"It is a remarkable fact, that the followers of this
religion worship an image with three heads and forty
hands, as a symbol of a Trinity of persons in the
godhead, and of the universality of the divine opera-
tions. They believe also that, whatever crimes may
have been committed, the sinner may expect salvation
if he dies invoking the Deity, whom they represent as
having undergone a most severe penance, in order to
wash away the sins of mankind. They also believe that
this God is invisible, and of a nature quite distinct
from the elements of matter; that he existed before the
creation of heaven and earth; that he had no beginning,
and will have no end; that all things were created by
him; that his essence is spread through the heavens,
upon the earth, and beyond it; that he is present everywhere; that he governs and preserves all things; that
he is immovable, immaterial, and ought to be reverenced as the inexhaustible source of all good."[1]

Similarities between Buddhism and Christianity
were noted by a visitor to Niigata, Japan, who wrote
in 1880: "On the whole, the Niigata temples are
ecclesiastical and devotional-looking, and if a few of
the Buddhist insignia were removed, they might be
used for Christian worship without alteration. Their
brass vessels are very beautiful, and their chalices,

[1] Captain Golownin, R.N. [Russian Navy], *Recollections of Japan*, London, 1819. Pp. 45-6.

flagons, lamps, and candlesticks are classical in form and severely simple. On the altars are draped standing figures of Buddha with glories round their heads, in gorgeous shrines, looking like Madonnas, and below them the altarpieces,... fresh flowers in the vases, and the curling smoke of incense diffusing a dreamy fragrance. Antique lamps, burning low and never extinguished, stand in front of the shrine. The fumes of incense, the tinkling of small bells, lighted candles on the high altar, the shaven crowns and flowing vestments of the priests, the prostrations and processions, the chanting of litanies in an unknown tongue, the 'chancel rail,' the dim light, and many other resemblances, both slight and important, recall the gorgeousness of the Roman ritual. From whence came the patterns of all these shrines, lamps, candlesticks, and brazen vessels, which Buddhist, Ritualist, Greek, and Romanist alike use, the tongues of flame in the temples, the holy water, the garments of the officiating priests, the candles and flowers on the altar, the white robes of the pilgrims, and all the other coincident affinities which daily startle one? Even the shops of the shrine-makers look like 'ecclesiastical decorations' shops in Oxford Street. Nor was the likeness lessened by the vast throng of worshippers telling their beads on their brown rosaries as they murmured their prayers, squatting on the matted floor of the great temple into which we went to hear the afternoon preaching. It was a very striking sight. The priestly orator sat on a square erection covered with violet silk, just within the rail. He wore a cassock of brocaded amber satin, a violet stole and hood, and a chasuble of white silk gauze, and held a rosary in his hand. A portion of the

Buddhist Scriptures lay on his lap, and from a text in this he preached with indescribable vehemence and much gesticulation, in a most singular, high-pitched key, painful to listen to. His subject was future punishment, i.e., the tortures of the Buddhist hells. When he came to the conclusion of the first part, in which he worked himself into the semblance of a maniac, he paused abruptly and repeated the words, 'Namu amida Butsu,' and all the congregation, slightly raising the hands on which the rosaries were wound, answered with the roar of a mighty response, 'Eternal Buddha, save.' Then he retired behind the altar, and the adult worshippers, relaxing their fixed attitudes, lighted their pipes and talked, and the children crawled about in the crowds. Then the priest, bowing as he passed the altar, took his place again on the rostrum, but before he began part two of his discourse, the prayer 'Eternal Buddha, save' murmured low through the temple like the sound of many waters, and so for two hours the service continued. Outside, under a canopy, the holy water stands.''[1]

When Devaki had given birth to the god Krishna, she learned that Kamsa had resolved to destroy the babe. Eluding the vigilance of the guards, she had Krishna secretly carried to the town of Gokulam, a motif which suggests the attempt of Herod to kill the babe Jesus, and the flight of the Holy Family to Egypt—a late introduction in the New Testament.

Vishnu, in the form of Krishna, is represented with a blue bee hovering over his head—a symbol of the

[1] Isabella L. Bird, *Unbeaten Tracks in Japan*, New York, 1880. Vol. I, pp. 12-15.

ether; and Christ is called "the Ethereal Bee." If the one belief did not influence the other directly, probably each derives from a common origin in Babylonian, Assyrian, or Mithraic, religion. This motif is the theme of an elaborate bas-relief on the south door of the baptistery of Parma. There a man is depicted sitting on the limb of a tree eagerly eating the honey which trickles from the leaves. At the foot of the tree is a dragon. Gnawing at the tree roots are two mice, one white and the other black, symbols of day and night and of the chief divisions of all-consuming Time which will eventually cause every tree of life to collapse. This motif has a counterpart in the India "Great Ocean of the Rivers Stories," in the tale of a traveler who fell asleep while up a tree in the forest. When he awoke he saw below him a tiger lying in wait, and above his head an enormous serpent coiled and ready to strike. On a branch by his side he discovered drops of honey from a swarm of bees in the hollow of the tree trunk. In his enjoyment of the honey he forgot his plight. This motif, which in India long antedates the legend inscribed at Parma, was incorporated in European tales, and presumably inspired the bas-relief at Parma. It appears in a thirteenth century French manuscript, now in the Pierpont Morgan Library:

"They that desire the delights corporeal and suffer their souls die for hunger, be like to a man that fled before a unicorn that he should not devour him and in fleeing he fell into a great pit, and as he fell he caught hold of a branch of a tree with his hands and set his feet upon a sliding place and then saw two mice, the one white and the other black, which without ceasing gnawed the root of the tree and had almost gnawed it asunder. And he saw in the bottom of this pit, an horrible dragon casting forth fire and who had his mouth open and desired to devour him .... Then he lifted up his eyes and saw a little honey that hung in the boughs of the tree and thereupon he forgot the peril that he was in and gave himself entirely to the sweetness of that honey.

"The unicorn is the figure of Death, which continually followeth man and desireth to seize him. The pit is the world which is full of wickedness. The tree is the life of every man, who, by the two mice that are day and night, and the hours thereof incessantly have been wasted and therefore approached to the cutting or gnawing asunder.... The horrible dragon is the mouth of hell which desireth to devour all creatures. The sweetness of the honey in the boughs of the tree is the false deceivable delectation of the world. By which man is deceived so that he takes no heed of the peril in which he is."

An Egyptian Vth dynasty illustration of the ceremony of "Opening the Mouth" depicts a calf, its left foreleg severed, walking in front of its mother. In front of the calf are two slaves; one bears the heart of the deceased in his hand, the other holds the left foreleg of the calf, which is apparently being placed on a table.

The custom here was to touch the mouth of the mummy with the foreleg of the sacrificial animal. The precise significance of the foreleg is not clear; there is, however, an analogy in a custom still in vogue in south India of placing the severed left foreleg of a sacrificed animal in the mouth of the severed head. The Toda, in their sacrifice of a calf, cut the left

foreleg, gather blood from it on a leaf, and burn this
in a fire. The Madiga of southeast India say that because a Madiga boy placed his hand on the breast of a
Brahmin woman, the right foot of a sacrificed buffalo
must be placed in its mouth as punishment.

The representation of Vishnu as a white horse in the
heavens with one foot upraised, suggests the attitude
of the Christian paschal lamb, which holds a cross
under an upraised forelimb. Another analogy with
Christianity is to be found in the importance attached
to the millennium which, in Japanese Buddhism, fixed
the date of Buddha's death at 949 B. C. The widespread
belief in the imminence of the millennium was based
on an old Buddhist legend which describes three
periods in the fortunes of the faith after Buddha's
death. During the first thousand years, the period of
the Perfect Law, monastic discipline will be strictly
observed. During the next thousand years, the period
of Copied Law, the true faith will decline, although
piety will be expressed in the founding of many temples
and monuments. The third millennium, the period of
the Latter Law, will last ten thousand years. It will be
a period of degeneration, in which vice and strife will
be rife. In Japan, the eleventh century seemed to fulfil
these predictions of the third millennium; many
believed that the prophecy was being fulfilled, and
some monastic orders proclaimed it. Saicho, who
founded the monastery of Hiei in preparation for the
coming age of degeneration, preached: ''Approaching
is the end of the Copied Law and nigh is that of the
Latter Law, and this is the time ripe for the propaga-
tion of the unique truth of the 'Lotus of Truth.' '' The
third millennium was near.

Closely related to this concept is the belief in the coming of the Buddha. In a Japanese book, *Birth in the Land of Purity*, written in 984, Genshin (Eshin Sozu), the "Abbot of Eshin-in," describes in near-Christian terms the reception of the soul of the faithful: "When a pious person dies, the Buddha appears before him. The Lord of Compassion [Kwannon], one of his Bodhisattvas, brings a lotus flower [on which] to carry the pious soul." The Lord of Might, Seishi, extends helping hands; hymns praising and welcoming the pious are sung by a multitude of saints and angels. The pious man is compared to a blind man who is born in the Land of Purity and is suddenly surrounded by radiant light and priceless jewels. Music fills the air, the sky radiates light, birds from heaven and from paradise fly about. Adoring creatures in paradise sing hymns in praise of Buddha. Some souls go to other lands where Buddha resides, some meditate serenely on pinions in the air. In the midst of these glories sits Amita Buddha, on a lotus compared to a golden mountain. Saints surround him. The newly-born soul is led to Buddha by the Lords of Compassion and of Might.

In Buddhism, as in Christianity, a bell is tolled at death. Buddhists believe that the tolling assists the departing spirit to cohere and solidify in the nebulous regions of the Intermediate State, that is to say, in Purgatory. In Christianity, the original purpose of tolling a bell at death was to frighten away evil spirits.

CHAPTER FIVE

Mariology and Mariolatry

THE name *Mary* as the Mother of Jesus first appears, in a possibly interpolated passage, in *Acts* (1:14), a manuscript written, at the earliest, some fifty to seventy years after the crucifixion. In cultures with which the early Christians had contacts this name was, in many instances, given to the mother of a great personage.

Adonis was the son of Myrrha; Hermes, the Greek *Logos*, was descended from Maia; Cyrus was the son of Marian (or Mandane); Moses, of Mariam; Joshua, according to the *Chronicle of Tabari*, of Mariam; Buddha, of Maya; Krishna, of Maritala; and in other instances *Mary*, or a linguistic variant, was the name of the mother of a god or of a great hero.

The motif of immaculate conception occurs in many regions in the Old World and the New. Plutarch places it in the time of Romulus. The Egyptian queen Hatshepsut, who became a ruling pharaoh, though known to be a daughter of the pharaoh Thutmose I, was declared to be a daughter of the god Amon-Re. The gods selected the queen-mother, "and it was recommended that Amon visit her while the pharaoh was still in his youthful vigor."

Among the Mother goddess cults prevalent in Mediterranean lands when Christianity came on the scene, none made a greater appeal than did that of Isis, perhaps in part because of representations of her with her infant son Horus. Devotion to Isis, "the sum of all deity, the Queen of Heaven," is expressed in the prayer of thanksgiving made by initiates into her cult: "O holy and blessed dame, the perpetual comfort of human kind, who by thy bounty and grace nourishest all the world, and bearest a great affection to the adversities of the miserable as a loving mother, thou takest no rest night or day, neither art thou idle at any time in giving benefits and succouring all men as well on land as sea; thou art she that puttest away all storms and dangers from men's life by stretching forth thy right hand, whereby likewise thou dost unweave even the inextricable and tangled web of fate, and appeasest the tempests of fortune, and keepest back the harmful course of the stars. The gods supernal do honour to thee; the gods infernal have thee in reverence; thou dost make all the earth to turn. Thou givest light to the sun, thou governest the world, thou treadest down the power of hell. By thy means the stars give answer, the seasons return, the gods rejoice, the elements serve; at thy commandment the winds do blow, the clouds nourish the earth, the seeds prosper, and the fruits do grow. The birds of the air, the beasts of the hill, the serpents of the den, and the fishes of the sea do tremble at thy majesty; but my spirit is not able to give thee sufficient praise, my patrimony is unable to satisfy thy sacrifices; my voice hath no power to utter that which I think of thy majesty, no, not if I had a thousand mouths and so many tongues and were able to continue for ever. Howbeit as a good religious person, and according to my poor estate, I will do what I may; I will always keep thy divine appearance in remembrance, and close the imagination of thy most holy godhead within my breast.''

The cult of Isis and Horus was followed in Egypt and neighboring countries by that of the Virgin Mary and the Child Jesus. Paintings and figures of Isis and of the Virgin Mary were made in Egypt as late as the fifth century A.D. The worship of Isis was introduced into Rome during the first century B.C. About 80 B.C. Sulla founded there an Isis College (community). Soon her temples were to be found in various parts of Italy and Western Europe, as far as London. She was worshiped until the fifth century, as a Lady of Sorrows weeping for the dead Osiris, and as a divine mother nursing her infant son Horus. She was closely associated with the mother goddess Cybele—that Mater Dolorosa whose mourning for her dead son Attis was celebrated annually in Rome at a shrine on the Vatican Hill, now the site of St. Peter's Church in which a cult of the Mother of God has long flourished.

This latter title was first applied to the Virgin Mary toward the end of the third century, by theologians in Alexandria, a renowned center of Isis worship. During the next century the designation became more frequent, and shortly before 400 Epiphanias denounced the women of various Eastern localities for worshiping Mary as a goddess and offering cakes at her shrine. However, about 430 we find Proclus hailing her as divine and calling her the Mother of God and mediator between God and man. The Feast of the Assumption, which celebrates the transportation of Mary to heaven by

Jesus and the angels, dates from the sixth century. It is celebrated on August 13, the date of the great festival of Diana (or Artemis), with whom Isis was identified. Before that, at the Oecumenical Council in 431, held in Ephesus, City of Diana, the Church first officially authorized the use of the phrase "Mother of God" as the designation for the Virgin Mary. This authorization was made in the heart of a region in which, for several hundred years, a Mother goddess had been an important deity.

The worship of the Blessed Virgin reached its apogee in the fifteenth century. In 1477 Pope Sixtus IV introduced into the Church calendar the festival of the Conceptio Immaculata. Mary, as the Bride of Christ and Mother of Christ, represents the Church: as Bride, she personifies eternity; as Mother, she is Defender of the Church. During that century the *Marienlied* became popular and widely known, and mariolatry was fraught with mysticism and symbolism. There was a reaction against this enthusiastic mariolatry in the sixteenth century when the laity revolted against such excessive devotionals. The new Protestant group, however, retained a certain traditional regard for the Virgin: in 1530, the Augsburg Confession described Mary as *"dignissima amplissimis honoribus,"* most worthy of honor.

In 1950 the bodily assumption of Mary into heaven became official Church doctrine. The Papal Allocution on the Doctrine of the Assumption, delivered in Latin October 30 of that year by Pope Pius XII to a Consistory of Cardinals and Bishops, and published in the official English translation on the following day, reads as follows:

"You well know the motive for which we have con-
voked this Sacred Consistory today. It is an event
which will fill us, you and the whole Catholic world
with unspeakable joy. On the first of November, the
Feast of All Saints, the radiant brow of the Queen of
Heaven and of the beloved Mother of God will be
wreathed with new splendor, when, under divine inspiration and assistance, we shall solemnly define and
decree Her bodily assumption into heaven.

"With the authority which the Divine Redeemer
transmitted to the Prince of the Apostles and to his
successors, we have the intention of ordaining and
defining what from the earliest days the Church piously
believes and honors, what the Holy Fathers have elabo-
rated and brought to a clearer light through the
centuries, and what the faithful of all classes everywhere have earnestly requested and implored by
innumerable documents—namely, that Mary the Virgin
Mother of God, was assumed, body and soul, into the
glory of heaven.

"Before taking this resolution, we deemed it oppor-
tune, as you are aware, to entrust the study of the
matter to experts. They, at our command, assembled
all the requests which had been addressed to the Holy
See on the matter, and examined them with all intention,
so that there might emerge, in the clearest possible
manner, what the Sacred Magisterium and the entire
Catholic Church held should be believed on this point
of doctrine.

"Furthermore, at our bidding, they studied with the
greatest diligence all the attestations, indications and
references in the common faith of the church regarding
the bodily assumption of the Blessed Virgin into

heaven, whether in the concordant teaching of the Sacred Magisterium, and in the Sacred Scripture and in the most ancient cult of the church, as well as lastly, in the writings of the Fathers and of the theologians and in the admirable harmony of this with other revealed truths.

"We also sent letters to all the Bishops requesting them to state not only their own opinion, but also the thought and desire of the clergy and faithful.

"In a wonderful and almost unanimous chorus, the voices of the pastors and of the faithful from every part of the world reached us professing the same faith and requesting the same things as supremely desired by all. We judged then that there was no reason for further delay, and we decided to proceed to the definition of the dogma.

"If it is true that the entire Catholic Church cannot deceive or be deceived, the Divine Redeemer, Who is truth itself, having promised to the Apostles: 'And behold, I am with you all days, even unto the consummation of the world,' it follows that this truth, firmly believed by the holy pastors and by the people, has been revealed by God, and can be defined by our supreme authority.

"Nor is it without the will of Divine Providence that this happy event should coincide with the Holy Year, which is now drawing to a close. It seems that to all and especially to those who from all parts of the earth came to this beloved city to purify their souls and renew their life in Christian practice, the Blessed Virgin Mary, resplendent on her throne as with a new light, stretched forth her maternal arms exhorting them to climb with courage the heights of virtue, so that, at the end of their earthly exile, they may come to the enjoyment of supreme happiness in their heavenly home.

"May the sublime Mother of God take under her watchful protection the innumerable multitudes, whom, with unspeakable joy, we have seen giving proof of fervent faith and ardent piety as they throng not only the house of the Common Father and the immense Basilica of St. Peter, but also the square of St. Peter and the adjoining streets, and may she obtain for them the heavenly lights and those gifts whereby they, illuminated and strengthened, may tend more readily to Christian perfection.

"Further, we nourish the great hope that the beloved Mother of God, crowned with new glory on earth, may contemplate with loving gaze and bind to herself those who languish in spiritual apathy, or slothfully dally in the snares of vice, or who, having lost the straight way of truth, do not recognize that sublime dignity of Hers, with which the privilege of her bodily assumption into heaven is strictly connected.

"May our most benign Mother, assumed to the glory of heaven, lead to that divine light, which descends only from on high, the entire human race which, in many places is still enveloped in the darkness of error, tormented by cruel chastisements and afflicted by grave dangers; may She obtain for them those supernal consolations which restore and raise up the soul of man, even if prostrate with frightful sufferings.

"May She obtain from her Divine Son that peace which is based, as on a most solid foundation, on the tranquillity of right order, on the just treatment of citizens and peoples, and on the liberty and dignity due to all, that it may finally return to shine among the nations and peoples at present divided to the common detriment.

"May She above all defend, with her most powerful patronage, the Catholic Church, which in not a few parts of the world is either little known or is charged with false accusations and calumnies, or oppressed by unjust persecutions; and may She lead back to the unity of the church all the erring and the wayward.

"Let you, venerable brothers, and with you the entire Christian people, strive to obtain all these things from the heavenly Mother by fervent prayer.

"But now, although, as we have said, the answers of the Bishops of all parts of the world have reached us on this matter, we desire nevertheless that you make your opinion to this thronged and august assembly also.

"Is it your good pleasure, venerable brothers, that we proclaim and define, as a dogma revealed by God, the bodily assumption of the Blessed Virgin into heaven?"

Having received the views of those present, expressed by "placet" or "non placet," the Pope went on:

"We greatly rejoice that all of you as with one thought and one voice assent to that which we ourselves think fitting and desire; because by this admirable agreement of the Cardinals and Bishops with the Roman Pontiff there emerges still more clearly what the Holy Church believes, teaches and desires in this matter.

"You will nevertheless kindly continue to implore God with unceasing prayer, so that, by His favor and inspiration, that which all ardently await may happily

come to pass; and may this event redound to the honor
of the Holy Name of God, to the benefit of the Christian
religion, to the glory of the Most Blessed Virgin, and
may it be for all a new incentive to piety toward her.''

On December 8, 1960, in the Piazza di Spagna at
Rome, Pope John XXIII, in observance of the Feast of
the Immaculate Conception, invoked a blessing and
placed a wreath of white chrysanthemums before the
statue of Mary in the square.

In 1958 St. John's University announced that it would
conduct an institute of Mariology on its Jamaica (New
York) campus, and that the courses for the program
would be open to graduate and undergraduate students,
the institute closing with a Marian convocation.

Religious ceremonies celebrated in 1963 at the
Marianapolis Preparatory School in Connecticut commemorated the 355th anniversary of the appearance of
the Mother of God at Shiluva, Lithuania. The occasion
was attended by an estimated one thousand devotees,
mainly of Lithuanian descent.

And some enthusiasts in Oaxaca, Mexico, not to be
outdone in manifestations of devotion, during the Feast
of the Assumption, fire heavenward a rocket bearing
a figure of the Virgin Mary well-rigged with fireworks.

CHAPTER SIX

Paganism in Christian Art and Symbolism

THE representation of cherubs as merely winged heads is reminiscent of Cretan seals which portray animal, or human, winged heads. It is also a reminder of Plato's concept of the *daimon* as complete in the head, with the body merely providing motion.

The Egyptians conceived the sun and moon as ships which transport the soul through celestial realms. Five thousand years ago a ship, first seen by archeologists in 1954, carried Cheops' soul to the sun, or to the sun god. About 3500 B.C. a model of a boat, fashioned from bitumen and with a cargo of clay vessels containing food, was placed on or alongside some graves at Ur in ancient Mesopotamia. Some archeologists interpret the British Bronze Age Beaker burial—in a coffin which has been hollowed out from the trunk of an oak tree, sometimes in the shape of a boat—as a reflection of the Egyptian concept that one passes to the next world over a water route. This idea took root in Scandinavia, where it developed into the great Viking ship-burials. Many of these British Food-Vessel people doubtless were sailors who traveled in dugouts to places overseas, and it could well be that ship-burials in England and Scandinavia had their own independent origins.

The Greeks believed that Charon used the winds to waft his boat, containing souls, far out over a stormy sea to the Isles of the Blest. And the ship was a feature of Dionysian festivals. At Smyrna in the second to third centuries A.D., according to Philostratos, a writer in that period, in the month of Anthesterion, a trireme with the priest of Dionysos at the helm was brought to the market-place from the high seas. A near-contemporary, the rhetorician Aristides, speaks of a trireme sacred to Dionysos being carried about the market-place in a circle. Centuries earlier, in the time of Pericles, the comic poet Harmippos referred to Dionysos as piloting his black ship over the wine-dark sea, bringing with him all kinds of good gifts for men.

The ancient Greeks compared the course of human life to the voyage of a ship, an imagery which was adopted by the early Christians. The ship is employed as a symbol in the decoration of several Christian tombs in the Roman catacombs, as well as in some of the tombs of early Christian Egypt. The *Apostolic Constitutions* of the late fourth century compares the edifice of the church to a ship. It shall be "long... and so it will be like a ship.... The deacons ... are like the mariners and managers of the ship," and the deacon is "as a manager of the foreship." Christian art depicts the boat as a conveyance of the soul, a concept appearing in Tennyson's *Crossing the Bar*:

"For though from out this bourne of time and space
   The flood may bear me far,
   I hope to see my Pilot face to face,
   When I have crossed the bar."

Early Christian illustrated manuscripts show an indebtedness to Jewish art, as do a group of paintings executed about the middle of the third century A.D. in the synagogue of Dura-Europos, a city in the Syrian desert about a hundred and fifty miles east of Palmyra, and situated on an ancient caravan route along the Euphrates. In later centuries the altar pictures, the sculpture in the aisles, and the architecture of the churches themselves, testify to Christian acceptance of artistic influences from many of the pagan cults against whose creeds Christianity was at war. In the fifteenth and sixteenth centuries the apparatus and accessories of Christian worship took on the colors and representations of pagan elements of the Renaissance, whereas the dogma, sacraments, basic rituals and organization of the Church remained essentially the same.

Mithraic temples had portrayals of Mithra shooting an arrow at a rock to bring forth water. Christian sculptors reproduced these as representations of Moses smiting a rock with a rod, and copied some accompanying Mithraic details.

In ancient Egypt a ray of light descended on the Sacred Cow, which thereupon conceived and bore the god Apis. Plutarch, in his treatise on Isis and Osiris, states that such conceptions take place through the ear. (Perhaps he was acquainted with the ancient Greek popular belief that the lizard conceives through the ear.) In Mesopotamia the ear, not the brain, was considered to be the seat of intelligence. In medieval pictures the Immaculate Conception is sometimes represented as a ray of light descending into Mary's ear.

The figure of Jesus carrying a lamb was inspired by statues of Hermes Kriophoros, the kid-carrying god, depicted carrying a ram; and Mithra is sometimes represented carrying a bull on his shoulders. On a sarcophagus in the Museo Pio-Clementino in Rome, the relief of a satyr bearing a lamb has features which strongly resemble those of the Christian Good Shepherd. Venus rising from the sea—"Venus on the Half-Shell" as it is sometimes called—became the Virgin Mary ascending to heaven. A striking example of this is the marble relief of the Assumption of the Virgin, originally in the Saint Jacques-la-Boucherie and now in the church of Saint Denis in Paris. Mary appears as a graceful figure, almost wholly nude, her hands folded in an attitude of prayer, with one foot on a cloud and the other on the head of a cherub. Four pagan genii, depicted as angels playing musical instruments, accompany her. Despite the Christian reinterpretation, the resemblance is to Venus rising from the sea rather than to Mary ascending to heaven.

In the year 800 the *Libri Carolini* observes that it is difficult to distinguish between images of Mary and Venus, unless they are labeled. When Captain John Saris visited Japan in 1613, the native Christians there took for a representation of the Virgin and Child a picture of Venus and Cupid which the captain had hanging in his cabin.

A Latin cross found in the ruins of Herculaneum and reported in 1939, indicates that the cross was used as a Christian symbol at least as early as 79 A.D., the year that Herculaneum was destroyed by an eruption of Mt. Vesuvius. However, the cross did not become a common Christian symbol until the time of Constan-

tine in the early fourth century, although it is much
older than Christianity itself.

Christian adoption of the cross was probably due to
pagan influences. In the most common form of cross
used by pre-Christian peoples—the Greek, or equilateral, cross—the four bars extending from the center
are of equal length. One of the oldest known examples
appears on an inscribed Babylonian cylinder-seal of
the Kassite period (1746-1171 B.C.). A wall-painting of
about 1250, from a tomb at Thebes, depicts two small
figures wearing an equilateral cross on the breast,
and there are other examples in the second millennium
B.C. Many small objects excavated at Troy by
Schliemann have an equilateral cross, as have prehistoric bronze vases and weapons in Scandinavia,
Germany, Austria, Switzerland, France and England.
Possibly it originally symbolized the heavens or a
celestial power, and later, divine protection, hence
prosperity, riches and life. In Assyrian sculptures
there is a solar, i.e. a radiating cross—the sun's disc,
from which four arms and four rays of light extend.
The arms probably represent the four quarters of the
heavens, over which the god Anu presides. A form of
the cross commonly designated Maltese, Coptic, or
rayed, is represented on the stele of the Assyrian king
Shashi-Adad VI (824-810 B.C.). In King's College
chapel of Cambridge University a stained-glass window
shows a garbed priest of the Temple of the Sun. Nearby
a figure holds in one hand an upright spear and in the
other hand a radiating solar disc in the center of which
a face is portrayed.

A hollow figurine of local clay from Bronze Age
deposits at Tell Beit Mirsim in Palestine represents

a naked woman pressing to her prominent breasts a dove with outstretched wings. Probably it symbolized fecundating power. In Palestine, Syria and Cyprus, the dove was sacred to the Semitic mother-goddess Astarte (Ishtar). It became a favorite symbol in Christian art, mainly because of its Old Testament associations.

CHAPTER SEVEN

Christian Feasts and Festivals

E ACH year the Egyptians celebrated the death and resurrection of Osiris. They mourned the dead god, lighting lamps outside the house in the evening and burning them throughout the night.

Plutarch says this festival was held about November 13. In ancient Egypt a feast for the dead was celebrated on or about November 8, soon after the beginning of their year (October 21). At this New Year's feast gifts were exchanged, some were given to the dead, and there was an illumination for the "glorification of the blessed." It was, in fact, a Feast of All Souls.

The festival of All Saints, November 1, stems from this Egyptian Osirian celebration. The Christian festival continues, but no longer commemorates, the worship of Osiris and the tribute to his subjects in the Kingdom of the Dead. In many countries, at the Christian Feast of All Souls (November 2) in honor of the dead, lamps and candles are burned throughout the night, a continuation of the Egyptian Feast of Lamps. The Church at first attempted unsuccessfully to suppress this pagan celebration, but officially recognized it in 998.

At the great festival of Dionysos, January 6, water turned into wine. Aristides Phetor states about 160 A.D.

that at the Egyptian celebration of this festival water was drawn from the Nile, because it was purest on that day, and was stored in wine-jars. With time it became sweeter, even as wine mellows with age. Clement of Alexandria says (about 194) that the Basilideans, an Egyptian sect of Gnostics, feasted on January 6, and otherwise celebrated the day. Soon the Christians in Syria and elsewhere were celebrating on this same day the anniversary of the baptism of Jesus in the Jordan. By the fourth century the ceremony was widely adopted; in 386 the celebration at Antioch included blessing all rivers and springs, after which water was drawn to be used throughout the year in baptismal rites.

The Roman Catholic Church commemorates on January 6 the turning of water into wine by Jesus at the Cana Marriage Feast. Epiphany (Twelfth Night), insofar as it is a commemoration of Jesus' baptism and of his turning water into wine, is a Christian continuation and reinterpretation of Dionysiac rites. In France there is the *gateau de la fève*, "bean cake," at Epiphany, during the Feast of the Three Kings. A cake in which a bean was baked is eaten on the evening of this Feast, and he who finds the bean in his piece is proclaimed King or Queen. Accounts of elaborate suppers sponsored by Louis XIV describe the practice of dispatching "ambassadors" by the "King" or the "Queen" of each supper-table to make alliances with fellow "sovereigns."

Several other Church festivals perpetuate paganism. The festival of St. George on April 23 continues the roman festival of the Parilia, the "Birthday of Rome." The festival of St. John the Baptist is a continuation of the midsummer water-festival in honor of Adonis or of another vegetation deity. The Church could not prevent people from rolling in the morning dew or bathing in a spring or river on that day, as a safeguard against future misfortune; accordingly it made the day sacred in memory of the Christian saint of waters, John the Baptist. The Feast of St. Peter in Chains (Lammas Day, August 1), is a continuation of the *Hláfmaesse*, or Bread Ceremony, an Anglo-Saxon festival of thanksgiving for the ripening of the grain.

The festival of Diana, under the Roman form of Vesta, was held August 13. At the feast there were wine, roasted kid, and clusters of apples still attached to the bough. This became the festival of the Assumption of the Blessed Virgin, celebrated on August 15, the season of ripening fruits, a time especially suitable for the worship of Diana. When Christianized Philippine rice-farmers celebrate a feast in honor of the Roman Catholic local saint, they set up a cross, sprinkle it with rice wine, and offer their devotions. The rice wine is a traditional offering to the native gods and the spirits of their ancestors, whom the Filipinos thus invite to share the food with them in spirit.

Spanish friars found that in Mexico, where there were many gods, the natives readily admitted new ones, giving them a place amid their aboriginal deities. In sacrifice, ritual and prayer these ''idols behind altars'' were cherished, and their images were placed alongside of or among those of the missionaries. Even when, as among the Tarascan Indians, their faith in the ancient gods waned, the concepts associated with them survived to be transferred to the images of the new gods, who now embodied the attributes of the old.

At a local festival of the Virgin Mary held about two decades ago in south Italy in mid-September, an effigy of the Virgin was carried in a procession through the village street. From baskets of wheat carried in their hands, peasants pitched wheat toward the Madonna in a silent plea for a bountiful harvest and good luck in general. This Madonna with a black face was actually a rescued deity of the underworld, a modern Persephone, treated as a goddess of the harvest. In front of some of the houses a table, over which a white cloth was laid, served as an altar. The paraders stood before them while the priest pronounced a blessing. Men and women then brought as offerings paper money, some of it dollar bills earned in the United States, and pinned them to the Virgin's robes.

Before their conversion to Christianity the Danes drank to Odin and Anses. They continued this ceremony after their conversion by devoting their offering to Jesus, the Apostles and the Saints. In early and medieval times the Church welcomed the transfer to Christianity of many heathen beliefs and practices, and some of these practices—such as the worship of wells and trees—persisted even after the Church forbade them. There were pagan dances by horned men at the January Calends. When misfortune threatened, or when Christian prayers proved to be of no avail, sacrifice was made to heathen gods. At marriage and at childbirth, women clung to pre-Christian customs long in vogue. To get the best of both worlds, in many instances the devout resorted to the ancient rites, often in secret. The Venerable Bede states that early in the seventh century there were two altars in the same temple, one devoted to Christian worship and the other available for sacrifice to the pagan gods. During the middle ages some witches confessed to adoring a pagan god: Marion Grant of Aberdeen, for example, confessed in 1596 that Christsonday was the name of her god, and that by his command she worshiped him on her knees.

CHAPTER EIGHT

Other Pagan Influences

CHRISTIANITY developed in pagan environments which influenced both the new faith itself and its forms of expression. Many concepts shared by heathens nourished the theologians and the devotees of Christianity. Both doctrine and ritual reflect, or refract, pagan sacred carnivals of remote antiquity, with their accompanying beliefs and practices. To the present day many Christian dogmas and liturgies carry evidence of their origin in a culture commonly called heathen—or worse.

Of these widely spread concepts none was farther flung than that of the trinity. In Taoist belief, Three produced all things. Ancient Near East theologians depict the cosmos as a "three-decker universe," a trinity composed of the sphere of the stars, the planets and the earth, the last-mentioned sphere extending to the moon. Each inferior world receives power from the adjacent superior world. The source of all force and virtue is in the highest sphere, one and indivisible. It regulates the entire universe.

Egyptians spoke of heaven, earth and Tuat (the deep). "All gods are three," reads an Egyptian text, "—Amon, Re, and Ptah—and they have no second." This triune being is one: "Amon and Re (and Ptah), together three.'' Re is the head; Ptah, the body; Amon, the name of this unity. The Egyptians had other trinities too: Osiris, Isis, Horus; Amen, Nut, Khensu; Khnum, Satis, Arinkis; Khepera, Shu, Tafnut; and others.

The Babylonians considered three, four, five, seven and fifteen to be lucky numbers. Three, symbolic of the trinity, was the most sacred. It symbolized birth, life, death; beginning, middle, end; childhood, manhood, old age. There were also triads of gods, such as Anu, Ea, Enlil (or Bel). After the fourteenth century B.C. the triad Sin, Shamash and Ashtar was identified with the moon, sun and Venus respectively, the moon god being the most powerful.

The ancient Greek trinity included Poseidon in the ocean, Zeus in the heavens, and *Aïdes* (Hades), ''who rules among those below the earth.'' Democritus groups the sun, moon and Venus, setting them apart from other heavenly bodies.

The same concept was familiar at Rome. Pliny describes Venus as ''the rival of the Sun and the Moon''; among the stars only Venus shines with such brilliance that her rays cast a shadow—a statement which, it has been observed, would be absurd in the climate of Rome, but which makes sense under the clear skies of Syria. Presumably, Pliny borrowed the description from an Eastern writer.

Classical myths depict a three-headed Cerberus, three Fates, three Furies, three Graces, three Harpies, three Gorgons and other trinities. The Pythagoreans, it is presumed, introduced into Greece the philosophic concept of the mystical significance of three. For Plato the three virtues—wisdom, courage

and moderation—correspond to the three parts of the
soul—intellect, will and emotion. In the fourth century
B.C. Aristotle observed: "All things are three, and
thrice is all: and let us use this number in the worship
of the gods; for, as the Pythagoreans say, everything
and all things are bounded by threes, for the end, the
middle, and the beginning have this number in everything, and these compose the number of the Trinity."

The Etruscan triad was Tima, Uni, Minerva; to them
the other gods gave precedence. The Teutonic triad
was Odin, Thor, Freyer. The Hindus have the great
trinity of Brahma, Siva and Vishnu. "These three
gods," Hindu books say, "are but one: Siva is the
heart of Vishnu, and Vishnu, the heart of Brahma; it
is one lamp with three lighted wicks." An early poet
of India wrote:

"In these three Persons the one God was shown—
Each first in place, each last—not one alone;
Of Brahma, Vishnu, Siva, each may be
First, second, third, among the blessed three."

The sacred thread which a Brahman initiate wears
over the left shoulder symbolizes this trinity. The
thread is composed of sets of three strands, each of
which has a set of three. They signify, respectively,
the triple nature of spirits; that of matter; and the
divine trinity or Trimurti of Brahma, Vishnu and Siva
(mind, speech and body), and the triple control over
them. The thread reminds the wearer of matters
concerning right living; it is a badge of his caste, a
guide to his actions. In the ancient north India creation
ritual there is a procession of animals: a horse,

symbolizing the nobility; an ass, symbolizing farmers and serfs; a male goat, who symbolizes priests.

Hinduism recognizes three elements or cosmic regions: earth, air and sky, each with its deity, Fire, Wind and Sun. Subsequently Wind, Sun and Moon are a trinity, and support the three worlds. In the Nilgiri Hills of south India the Kota triad is Elder Father God, Younger Father God and Mother God. The Buddhist Precious Triad, the Sanskrit *Triratna*, consists of Guatama (the founder of Buddhism), the Law and the Priesthood. The early Japanese divine trio was Sun, Moon and Rainstorm.

Both the Old and the New Testament contain many instances of the use of three as a symbolic, or perfect, number. God called Samuel three times; David bowed before the Lord three times; three times Jesus asked Peter whether he (Peter) loved him; the Magi were three in number. (According to one legend they were twelve.) On the way to Golgotha Jesus fell down three times.

Probably the concept of a three-plane universe, common to most tribal peoples the world over, and to early Mediterranean and Indo-Iranian cultures, was the ultimate source of the concept of the Trinity adopted by Christianity. The Trinity is not mentioned in the New Testament, nor is it referred to in the earliest formulated articles of the faith, the Apostles' Creed. Apparently it is a later Mediterranean inspiration. St. Justin, St. Clement, Theodoret, St. Augustine and other early Church Fathers, prove the truth of the mystery of the Trinity by citing Greek philosophers as authorities, particularly Plato and his disciples Plotinus and Porphyry, in whose writings the words

Father, *Son*, *Word* (or *Spirit*) occur. The *Father* comprehended perfection; the *Son* was the perfect image of the *Father*; and by the *Word* were all things created; these three were one God.

The earliest surviving representation of the crucifixion dates from about 430 (in the church of Santa Sabina in Rome). The motif is not one of the most ancient in known Christian art. Until the twelfth century Jesus was represented as fastened to the cross with four nails, one in each hand and foot; then, in deference to the doctrine of the Trinity, he was represented with one foot resting over the other, and three nails were shown. Cimabue, who first used this style, was twenty years old when, in 1260, the Synod of Arles directed that the Feast of the Holy Trinity be celebrated.

The Roman Catholic Church defines the trinity of man as consisting of three parts: body, soul and spirit. In the after-world there are three regions: heaven, hell and purgatory. In Church architecture there is the three-light window, and in Christian art the trefoil, or triangle, usually symbolizes the Trinity. The Church itself is threefold: a Church militant, a Church suffering, a Church triumphant.

The triple papal crown (the triregnum), is of white fabric, dome-shaped, and covers the head. It contains three crowns, and in addition is surmounted by a crown and a globe. Formerly the Pope wore it when he rode a white mule to St. John Lateran, in cavalcade, and took possession of the basilica. Tradition states that it was first worn, as a "camelauco," by the Syrian Pope Constantine, who held office from 708 until 715. This "camelauco" is believed to have come from the

East. A gold band extended around the bottom of this headdress. In the first half of the tenth century this band had the form of a crown, designated a "regnum," a reign, symbolizing the sovereignty of the Pope.

Early in the fourteenth century Pope Boniface VIII wore two crowns, and the tiara was therefore called a "bi-regnum." A third crown was added a few years later, either by Benedict XI or Clement V.

The symbolism of three in European folklore is illustrated in the *Kalevala*, a medieval Finnish collection of heroic poetry:

> "Thence arose three mighty rivers
>
> . . . .
> From each stream that thus was fashioned,
> Rushed three waterfalls in fury,
> And amid each cataract's flowing,
> Three great rocks arose together,
> And on every rocky summit
> There arose a golden mountain,
> And on every mountain summit
> Up there sprang three beauteous birch-trees,
> In the crown of every birch-tree,
> Golden cuckoos three were perching."

In January 1893 a clergyman published in *The Dublin Review* an article on "Vestiges of the Blessed Trinity in the Material Creation," wherein he set forth that this doctrine is "written large across the whole face of nature," in "such familiar things as rocks, mountains, seas, and lakes." As evidences of the "mystery of the Trinity" he reminded that every object has three dimensions; a plant is composed of seed, stalk

and flower; life is "vegetative, sensitive, and ra-
tional"; matter is solid, fluid or gaseous; time is
present, past or future; there are "three fundamental
colors," which dissolve in the unity of white—"light-
red, yellow, and blue." And so on, with many more
illustrations of naturalistic trinitarianism.

Sir William Hamilton—quoting[1] from an account in
the *Intellectual Powers* of one "Dr. Reid," tells of a
musician who thought that "there could be only three
parts in a harmony—to wit, bass, tenor, and treble;
because there are but three persons in the Trinity."
And if Andrew Lang's pleasantry[2] can be accepted as
fact, a preacher "demonstrated the existence of the
Trinity thus: 'For is there not, my brethren, one sun,
and one moon,—and one multitude of stars?'" One
suspects that Jesus and the authors of the books of the
New Testament would have been perplexed by some of
the concepts and practices which during the centuries
have found their way into some Church doctrine. One
suspects, too, that if those same Jews attended a
twentieth century church service they would not be
invited to take a front pew.

In the sanctuary of the Latin goddess Vesta, Vestal
Virgins nourished perpetual fire. In the fourth century
B.C., when Pytheas of Massilia visited Britain, he
landed on the island of Azantos (Uxisana), now called
Ushant, and there visited a temple in which nine Gaelic
priestesses maintained a perpetual fire in honor of
their god. In the twelfth century Giraldus states that a

[1] In *Lectures on Metaphysics and Logic*, Edinburgh &
London, 1859.
[2] In *Custom and Myth*, London, 1893.

perpetual fire was kept at a shrine of St. Bridget at Kildare. "Each of her nineteen nuns has the care of the fire for a single night in turn, and on the evening of the twentieth night, the last nun, having heaped wood upon the fire, says, 'Bridget, take charge of your own fire, for this night belongs to you.' She then leaves the fire, and in the morning it is found that the fire has not gone out, and that the usual quantity of fuel has been used." This sacred fire was maintained continually until the time of Henry VIII, who suppressed the monasteries. Formerly, in Scotland perpetual fire was kept in at least three monasteries.

The concept of eternal hell-fire, presided over by Satan, appears to have come into Christian belief after 100 A.D. Jesus apparently did not believe in a personal devil, although he believed in the powers of evil. The concept of the Prince of Darkness probably came from Mithraism. Satan is the Iranian Ahriman, eternal enemy of Ormazd; he may also be the ancient Egyptian Seth, opponent of Osiris. The devil as Mephistopheles is, it seems, derived from the once beloved god Pan. As Beelzebub he is Zeus Myiagros, Disperser of Flies, a benevolent god and a patron of flocks. Philistines at Ekron called him Ba'al-z-bub, Lord of Flies.

In the sixth century Gregory of Tours describes an annual ceremony held by pagan Gauls on Mount Helanus, in the district of Geraudan, Lozère; there, during a three-day festival, the inhabitants threw into the lake at the summit of the mountain offerings of cloth, skins, cheese, wax, bread, and anything else they could afford. On the fourth day, at the hour of resuming normal routine, there was a violent storm accompanied by thunder, lightning and sleet. In the third century, after the introduction of Christianity, a local bishop built on the shore of the lake a church in honor of St. Hilaire of Poitiers, who was efficient in calming storms. Thus the bishop converted a pagan cult into sanctified Christian practice.

In the early eighteenth century a similar annual custom was in vogue in the region of Foix, Ariège, at a deep lake on Mount Thabor, on which stood a church dedicated to St. Bartholomew. On August 24 a crowd assembled to celebrate mass in the chapel, and at an outdoor altar. Cinders were spread on the altar and the name *Jesus*, or another name, was traced in them. The ashes, it was said, would be found intact the following year, thus demonstrating that the summit of Mount Thabor was above the region of wind and rain. Even so, if one should stir up this lake of Saint Bartholomew, a violent storm accompanied by thunder and lightning would immediately ensue. This practice of spreading cinders on the altar may have been a survival of a pagan sacrifice.

Ancient Germanic tribes venerated stones, and employed them as periapts (charms). In a forest in the Deister, Germany, is a rocky place called Devil's Dancing-ground. Legend says the large flat stone there, in which there is a chiseled groove, formerly was used in connection with sacrifices. Early Christian priests utilized this "Christening stone" as a baptismal font.

In 452 the Council of Arles decreed that "if, in any diocese, any infidel lighted torches or worshiped trees, fountains, or stones, he should be [adjudged] guilty of sacrilege." From the fifth to the eleventh century the

Church intermittently issued edicts prohibiting the worship of stones or making offerings to them, which prohibition, of course, implies the practice.

In 1349 the Earl of Ross and the Bishop of Aberdeen met at the standing-stones of Rayne. In 1380 Alexander, "Wolf of Badenoch," commanded the Bishop of Moray to meet him at the Rait standing-stones. The Bishop, "standing inside the circle," protested against the proceedings. Some of the stones and rocks in Derbyshire are wayfarers turned to stone during the Great Frost of the early seventeenth century. In parish Mochrum, in Scotland, it is unlucky to cart away "standing-stones," that is, stones of so-called Druid circles.

In Västerhejde, on the island of Gotland, Sweden, there is a well-known custom in connection with the *Gladajk*, or *Gladek* (Glad Oak). Passers-by throw two or three stones into the hollow trunk of the tree and say: "Glad Oak, good progress!" Gotland coins of about 1310 to 1510 have an armorial design, usually designated as a lily. On seventy of the eighty known specimens the lower portion terminates in a triple root, as do seals from the island. On a Visby municipal seal, three birds sit on the branches of a "lily," the root of which is in three parts, the top terminating in a cross. Many medieval gravestones on Gotland have this design, and it decorates parts of churches, as for example a choir pew in Gothem church. It probably represents not a lily but a sacred oak, the tree of life, which tree still appears on the seals of some Gotland clergy.

The bodies of birds of prey which were hung over the doors of stables and cowbarns in Scandinavia, were originally offerings to Odin. The raven, daw, and magpie were holy because these scavengers ate corpses. Killing one of them brought misfortune. After the introduction of Christianity their bodies, wings outspread and forming a cross, were nailed to a building.

The rosary, "counting" beads while performing devotions, was presumably borrowed from the Mohammedans in the second decade of the thirteenth century. The Dominicans introduced it to keep account of prayers. The custom is derided in a stall carving in the Cleves Minorite cloister (dated from 1474), which shows an ass wearing a rosary.

The fact that the word *baldachin*, the designation for the canopy borne in processions and placed over an altar or other sacred object, is derived from the word *Bagdad* suggests Mohammedan origin. The silk from which it was made came from Bagdad. However, the early history of the baldachin is obscure.

The social status assigned to members of human societies was sometimes bestowed on animals. At the celebration of the Mass of the Dogs at Chantilly, on St. Hubert's Day, the oldest nobleman, mounted on the oldest horse, followed by the oldest dog and accompanied by the oldest groom, led a procession of dogs to the Mass. Behind them followed: the high dignitaries of the kennels, the convocation of nobles, and the general assembly of German bulldogs with round heads, clipped ears, collars bristling with iron spikes. After them: the great greyhounds with cropped hair, nervous legs, drooping bellies, muzzles like a marten's; all varieties of the long-haired; greyhounds; dogs mixed with spaniel; setters, who bounded about; harp-shaped

beauties, apparently without bellies; noble greyhounds,
with wide backs; greyhounds with black palates; and
others. In sixth place came a deputation of pointers,
with ears of extreme dignity. Then the bloodhounds;
next the bassets, terror of badgers, which respond to
the command, "Run, run, basset!" After them came
all pedigreed hounds or French dogs. Then the squint-
eyed, the scavengers, tramps, gossips, mastiffs, and
the dogs of brains and enterprise known as bawlers—
in short, the canine rabble. They were brought in this
order to the center of the chapel where they were
arrayed before the painting of St. Hubert and the Mass
began.

CHAPTER NINE

Missionary Christianity

INSISTENCE on tolerance and on adaptation to local demands pervades the admonition of Gregory the Great (540-604) to missionaries sent to England to convert the heathen to Christianity. Although they were not to yield on essential points, they should do everything possible to ignore minor differences, and they were not to shock heathen religious sentiments unless absolutely necessary. The heathen temples were to be adapted to Christian churches; the ancient heathen feasts were to be retained, but as a form of thanksgiving to God rather than a sacrifice to devils. In adapting the temples to churches, they should first be sprinkled with holy water and then outfitted with altars and Christian relics. In such manner the natives would continue to repair to their familiar temples as holy places, now to worship the true God in place of their former heathen idols.

Gibbon says that at the end of the fifth century a certain Saxon bishop urged that arguments for the faith be given with temper and moderation, in order to make the unbelievers ashamed without making them angry. This attitude is reminiscent of the stand reportedly taken by the Burmese Buddhist king, A-naw-ra-hta. When asked why he tolerated pagan *Nat* images in a Buddhist shrine, he replied: "Men will not come for the sake of the new faith. Let them come for their old gods and gradually they will be won over." His confidence was justified. In Burma, Buddhism has to a considerable extent prevailed over the entrenched pagan animism. Human sacrifice is not practiced, and animal sacrifice is made only furtively or in clandestine circumstances—all of which demonstrates that there is some reward for tempering the winds of doctrine to the shorn lamb.

The sixteenth century Jesuit missionary, Father Matteo Ricci (1552-1610), who labored in China, believed that if Christianity was presented to the Chinese in a manner which accorded with their own traditions, it would be accepted. So he entered China under the name of Li Ma-t'ou, which sounded Chinese; he wore at first the drab gray dress of a Buddhist priest, but later discarded it in favor of an impressive silk robe of purple, with magnificent adornments. His knowledge of mathematics and astronomy, and his proficiency in the Chinese literary language, together with his princely manners and bearing, earned him a respectful hearing at the court of the Emperor.

Over a century ago the Abbé J. A. Dubois expressed his strong disapproval of the offensive actions of some Christians against the Jains, a heterodox Hindu cult. The Christians entered the Jains' sacred ground, taking their dogs with them, and cooked their beef before the local idol who, the Jains were convinced, must have found such abominable cooking odors to be a stench in the nostrils. There was no excuse, the Abbé insisted, for any missionary to outrage the local sentiments of those whom he hoped to convert, no matter how strange

or unreasonable such sentiments might appear to be.
And he quoted the great skeptic, Voltaire, as a bad
example: "Did Cambyses do well, when after his
conquest of Egypt, he killed the ox Abis with his own
hand? Why not? He showed the idiots that their gods
could be brought to the pit without nature rising in her
wrath to avenge the sacrilege!" No wise statesman,
the Abbé observed, would share this opinion today.

In a similar vein the Anglican Canon T. K. Cheyne
observed in 1886 about Christian missionary efforts
among the Mohammedans: "If we ridicule the super-
stitions of their time-honoured beliefs, we on the one
hand increase their prejudice against the Gospel, and
on the other fail to understand the beliefs which we
oppose.... The word 'superstitious' never crossed the
lips of the Apostle to the Gentiles." Such attitudes as
these are sounder psychology than the disposition to
uproot everything historically non-Christian. Indeed,
recent missionary Christianity in foreign lands is in
part a story of adaptation of doctrine to local needs and
prejudices, and frequently it has incorporated some
traits of the local culture into the faith it comes to
preach.

Christian missionary priests among the Cheremis
of east central Russia gave their prayers a pagan
format and sought to identify Christian figures with
pagan deities, in an effort to induce the Cheremis to
accept Christianity. The Cheremis responded readily
enough (perhaps too readily) by incorporating the
Christian God and saints into their own formidable
catalogue of pagan deities. The result was that they
frequently lost sight of the distinction between their
pagan gods and the Christian one, and in some cases

found it necessary to consult a local seer to advise them whether a particular prayer should best be addressed to a Christian or a Cheremis god.

In early Connecticut it was an almost universal custom, known as "dignifying the meeting," to assign church pews each year according to the relative importance, rank, or status, of members of the parish. In many English village churches the communion is taken by social rank, a practice which was also observed in India in the churches of Hindu converts to Christianity. Although Christianity preaches equality of all men before God and in the Church, in India it has not been possible to dispense with caste separatism among Christianized natives, at least as regards the depressed caste, the "untouchables." In the (English) Established Church of India a partition wall, or a railing along the aisle, separated "untouchables" from higher castes. In some localities there were two churches—at opposite ends of the village—for the two groups. A few years ago a new pastor attempted to have everyone sit together without distinction, with the result that members of the higher castes returned to Hinduism. In south India, however, members of the depressed castes who had adopted Christianity, started the "self-respect movement" in an attempt to abolish such caste distinctions. We need not go to India, however, to find such distinctions and their inevitable resentments, in "Christian" churches.

During the last hundred years and more, with the exception of the Leipzig Missionary Society of South India—which considered castes to be merely a distinction in rank similar to those of the English country churches—there has been a strong inclination to do

away with caste distinctions among Indian converts to
Christianity, not without considerable local objection.
In south India, despite the insistence by an Anglican
Bishop that such separation was a violation of the
spirit of Christianity, higher castes refused to take
communion with lower ones. At the communion table
Sudras took precedence over Pariahs. The latter sat
as a separate group in the church, and were buried
apart from the graves of members of a higher caste.
When this same Anglican Bishop ruled in 1833 that
distinctions of caste would no longer be tolerated in
the Church, the Sudras of one congregation cancelled
their membership in a body, catechists resigned by the
hundreds, and the Government in India was deluged with
petitions and memorials by the higher castes who
objected to taking communion with the lowly, mean
Pariahs who swept the streets and handled corpses.
Despite the continuing efforts of Christian missionaries since then, such caste separatism still persists
today in Christian churches of India.

Christianity has its "Brahmins," a large group of
professing Christians on the Malabar coast who claim
descent from converts made by the Apostle Thomas in
the first century A.D. They practice the rites of the
Syriac Church, and look down on more recent converts,
refusing to admit them to the fold. The Hindus consider
them to be a rather high caste. At the bottom of the
scale are the Christian depressed classes, the untouchables. Between these two are Christians who claim
descent from converts made by Portuguese or French
missionaries two to four centuries ago. In deference
to native feelings, barriers are erected in the churches,
with the untouchables on one side and the Christians of

caste on the other, each group out of sight of the other. In Christian churches in Korea, where men and women may not associate in a gathering, a similar solution was found by placing the sexes on opposite sides of the church with a curtain between them to shut off their view of one another, while the preacher stood in the middle of an elevated pulpit where he could see and be seen by all.

Among the Madiga—a leather-workers caste in southeast India—Christian missionaries incorporate certain elements of pagan rites in the wedding service. The bridegroom ties a small gold disc around the neck of the bride, signifying his acceptance of her as a wife. Friends of the bridge and groom offer them presents which they had received at their own marriage ceremonies, thus defraying the expenses of weddings in accord with an old Madiga custom.

The Jews in Cochin (southwest India) constitute three castes, and consequently have had problems similar to those of the Indian Christians, with the members of the lowest cast—the so-called "black Jews"—making strenuous efforts to abrogate the old caste lines.

Adoptions and adaptations by Christianity have not been limited to the early period of its history, but have continued to the present day. This is notably so in Latin America and among the Pueblo peoples in the southwest United States who, in the seventeenth century, were under the influence of Spanish missionaries. Among the eastern Pueblos the pantheon of supernaturals was augmented, not replaced. Patron village saints were accepted, and these local cults contain native as well as Catholic rituals.

At Capacabana, on Lake Titicaca, there was in the sixteenth century a shrine which served as the center of an elaborate cult and which the Indians periodically visited in large numbers. Christian missionaries substituted a cult of the Virgin Mary at this shrine, and built a church there. In Kauri village (Department of Cuzco, Peru) each morning when the first rays of the sun appear, Quichua men stand outside the house, bow the head, and with hat in hand, pray to the "Most Holy Virgin Mary, Sun, young, powerful" to give them a good day free of troubles.

Among the Aymara of Bolivia, Jesus is the Creator, sometimes is God, but is not the traditional Christian Jesus. Before he came to the world it was lighted only by the moon and was dominated by divinities dwelling on mountain peaks. Jesus burned these divinities and thus freed the land for settlement by its present inhabitants. Apparently he has been substituted for the sun in this revised myth of the cataclysm. As for the Virgin Mary, they identify her with their traditional earth-goddess. However, it is difficult for the Aymara to believe that the Lady introduced to them by blood-thirsty conquerors possessed the all-merciful attributes which the missionaries ascribed to her. They are inclined to transfer to her the tradition of violence associated with their conquerors. A crime committed on Good Friday—except for murder—will go unpunished by the deity, for on that day God was dead.

Several native fiestas which fall on a date close to that of a Christian celebration are merged with the latter. Among the Aymara in southern Peru, and to some degree among the Maya in Santa Eulalia, God and the saints were merged with personages of the aboriginal religion, and virtually lost their identity in the process; little thought is given to the Christian God, and the Virgin is a remote figure to them, while the saints are ranked along with the native mountain spirits, the homage they receive being limited mainly to public feast days.

In Mexico the natives found many similarities between their ancient beliefs and those introduced by the Spaniards, and a successful amalgamation was accomplished without much difficulty. Catholic priests found that they could not abolish native Maya celebrations, so they simply substituted comparable Catholic ones, some of which came at about the same time of the year. The result was that some of the Indians came to adopt the Christian introductions as aboriginal ceremonies.

Among the Papago of northern Mexico and Arizona a sacred native dance, attended by much clowning, was encouraged and utilized by missionaries as a vehicle for presenting Christian tenets in a familiar and dramatic setting. It was still being sponsored by the Church in 1946, and frequently includes a dance performed by natives wearing a non-Indian garb called *fariseos*—that is, Pharisees.

Among Mestizos in Latin America, Roman Catholicism exhibits several traits more typical of the religion of south Europe than of that of north Europe or the United States. Almost everywhere these include certain supernatural beliefs and practices which are in part aboriginal, and in part persistences from the Middle Ages.

In 1935 at least seventy cults in Salvador, Bahia, Brazil, contained religious concepts mainly West

African, and now combined with concepts of Portuguese Catholicism. They include the African deity of
lightning, Xango; the god of war and of iron, Ogun; the
divinity of wind, Yansan; the god of the hunt, Oxossi.
A small fetish idol represents, respectively, each of
them, and each of these African deities is now conceived as a Christian saint. Thus Yansan has become
Santa Barbara; Ogun is now San Antonio, and Exu, the
African god of evil, is merged with our Devil. Several
of the cults are led by so-called Mothers of the
Saints, and the superior head of a cult is usually called
Father of the Saint. For the most part the religious
leaders are old people versed in the rituals and
behavior of the deity of the cult. As a rule a vaulted
straw hut is the local temple, with smaller structures
around it containing altars to the deities and serving
as shelters for the leader and a small retinue of his
followers. Each cult has its special ceremonial season,
and special days are consecrated to all the deities
together.

In northeast Brazil on January 1 Mass is celebrated
in the fishermen's chapel. The priest goes to the beach
and blesses the canoes. Members of African cults then
make their presents to the Mother of Waters. These
consist of money, or anything that a woman can use,
provided the object is white—comb, ribbon, powder,
perfume, soap, or other such things. The priestess of
the cult, accompanied by participants and onlookers,
goes to the beach and enters a large canoe which has
been prepared for her. The canoes go up the river, to
the sound of beating drums and singing devotees, who
call to the Mother of Waters and sing her praises. At
the dwelling place of the younger Mother of Waters,

presents are lowered into the water. If they fail to sink, the presents have been rejected—a very bad omen. If they sink, the Mother of Waters enters the person who placed the gift on the water.

In Haiti, St. Anthony has taken over the role of Legba, the trickster god of Dahomey and Yoruba, in West Africa. Legba was conceived as a wandering old man clad in tatters, so St. Anthony is now a patron of the poor. And there are several other comparable substitutions of this nature.

Christianity appealed to some groups of Dakota Indians because it promised a heaven similar to that depicted by the Dakota for their dead. On the Yakima reservation in the state of Washington the Indians have adapted Christmas to their native potlatch and long-house ceremonies, native chants and dances alternating with Christmas carols. The potlatch, at which gifts were given to guests, was neatly and easily fitted into the Christmas tradition. The agent on the Makah reservation sought to prohibit the celebration of a potlatch, but one of the local Indians found an eminently satisfactory and respectable solution; he celebrated his potlatch at Christmas time by hanging his goods on a Christmas tree and giving them away as presents, with the blessing of both the agent and the resident missionary.

In order to make their message more effective to the Indians, missionaries in the Puget Sound region designated their sacraments as "medicines," giving them a magico-religious character with which the Indians were familiar. Most tribal peoples have difficulty in understanding various aspects of the Christian message as delivered by missionaries. For example, the Shakers of northwest North America—in no way related to the Shakers of the Eastern states— were, for the most part, perplexed and mystified by missionary accounts of the Trinity, communion, baptism and hell. Nor were they able to unravel such subtleties as sin, salvation, confession, Christian love, or the millennium. So they simply gave up trying and concluded that what they could not understand could not therefore have any meaning and was ridiculous, a feeling which manifested itself regularly in the schools conducted by their white mentors.

In tribal cultures, as in more advanced societies, rival denominationalism can be a divisive force. Nearly a century ago a Nez Percé chief opposed the introduction of a Christian church among his people. He did not want them to quarrel about God, he said, as the Catholics and Protestants do. His people sometimes quarreled among themselves about mundane things, but never about God, and he begged that they not be led to add that to their troubles.

In 1930 an Australian Government anthropologist, reporting on the activities of the Siuai of Bougainville, observed that the competitive exhortations of Roman Catholic and Methodist missionaries were leading the natives into a frenzy of excitement not seen since the old days of inter-tribal warfare. He suggested that the Government intervene to prevail upon the rival missionary groups to work out some arrangement for a more seemly conversion of the natives.

In 1956 a missionary to an African tribe claimed that she could get closer to the natives in ten minutes by taking part in their tribal dance than she could ever hope to do with hours of sermonizing. The

Seventh Day Adventist mission countenances the practice of circumcision in the initiation ceremonies and
also, with some misgivings, clitoridectomy. In East
Africa a Bishop of Masai, believing that abolition by
missionaries of native initiation ceremonies might be
detrimental to the natives, purged the native rites of
their most objectionable practices and reinterpreted
the remainder from the Christian point of view. A
cross supplanted the phallic tree, saints were invoked
in place of tribal heroes, the dances were expurgated,
and Holy Mass and circumcision concluded the proceedings. During the period of seclusion, Christian
teachers gave instruction in manliness; this was then
completed with confession, head-shaving, donning of
new clothes, burning of old staffs, and in a Mass of
Thanksgiving, the censing of each boy as a potential
bridegroom, after which he was restored to his waiting
mother at the door of the church. Similar changes
were made in the tribal initiation ceremony for girls,
with women missionaries giving instruction regarding
marriage and motherhood.

An earlier missionary, in adapting Church methods
to the social framework of the Chaga of Tanganyika,
based sponsorship on kinship and gave sponsors the
authority to supervise matters concerning the proper
Christian conduct and discipline of their wards. So
thoroughly did he ritualize neighborhood, age-group
and eldership, that members of the congregation were
bound to each other in a network of the most elaborate
ceremonial relationships.

Matteo Ricci, the Italian Jesuit missionary who
labored in China in the late sixteenth and early
seventeenth centuries, took scrupulous care not to jar

the delicate susceptibilities and sense of propriety of the Chinese among whom he lived. He was convinced that Christianity could not succeed in China unless it conformed to Oriental patterns of thought, and took to itself the best features of a civilization which, he believed, was older than the culture in which Christianity was nurtured.

At least one church in China uses an amalgam of Christian and native marriage ceremonies, combining traits common to each and eliminating elements offensive to either. It includes giving presents, which is common to both; it also incorporates the Chinese customs of a "go-between," the exchange of betrothal cards, sending of betrothal presents, signing of the marriage contract by the two families, a procession in which the bride is borne to the home of the groom in a red chair, and reception of the bride by the groom in his home, where the celebrations are held. The Chinese worship of Heaven, Earth and the ancestors of the wedded couple are omitted. There are vows of reverence and respect, and a minister officiates. The giving of a ring and the holding of hands are omitted because they violate Chinese standards of propriety and dignity.

Church societies today are increasingly aware of the need for circumspection in matters sociological and anthropological if missionary work is to succeed. The "Conclusions and Recommendations" issued at the close of the 1957 conference of Canadian supervisors of Catholic schools for Indians calls for a school program which recognizes the special nature of the Indian's ethnic and cultural background. A Protestant Board of Missions report of 1962 included a college degree plus appropriate professional training as a necessary qualification for missionary work. And in a recent (1961) issue of the *Anthropological Quarterly*, Louis J. Luzbetak, who spent four years as a missionary with the Middle Wahgi of central New Guinea, emphasizes from personal experience the importance of a knowledge of the entire culture. The mistake, he says, is "not so much in not being interested in the culture *as a whole*, as a more or less single, integrated entity.... Culture is ... like a living organism whose parts cannot be understood except in relation to all other parts. Applied Missionary Anthropology would seek approaches to evangelization that would be based on this functional and organized view of culture.... [The] approach or policy would be as good as [one's] grasp of the interwebbing of cultural parts.... To an American, a pig is nothing more than a potential sausage or canned ham and a source of income for certain individuals. To the New Guinea native the pig is incomparably more, for the animal is intermeshed with practically every aspect of native life."

CHAPTER TEN

Christmas Spirits

Some say that ever 'gainst that season comes
Wherein our Saviour's birth is celebrated,
This bird of dawning singeth all night long,
And then, they say, no spirit dare stir abroad,
The nights are wholesome, then no planets strike,
No fairy takes, nor witch hath power to charm.
So hallowed and so gracious is that time.

HAMLET, Act I, Scene I

SHAKESPEARE to the contrary, the dark period of the pagan winter solstice moon, when evil forces stalked abroad, was transferred to the Christmas season in many parts of Europe. All sorts of beings become active at this time: angels and brownies visit Scandinavian homes on Christmas night, where the table is set with food for them; in Finland, bread, cheese, butter, whiskey, and an occasional ham or leg of mutton are left on the Christmas table throughout the holidays for the nourishment of hosts of unseen guests; in Lithuania a vacant chair is set at table for recently deceased members of the family, and food is left on the table throughout the night for the souls of long dead ancestors. In Sweden, liquor and the season's treats are left in the cemetery at night; at that time the dead rise and celebrate their *julotta*, and anyone who is bold enough to go to the church in the dark hours before the early Christmas morning service, will hear his ancestors singing and see long-dead pastors saying Mass or preaching.

Satan himself, exasperated by the beneficent influence of the holy season on mankind, doubles his malevolent energies at Christmas time, and special precautions must be made against him. In the Province of Berry (France), at nightfall on Christmas Eve the doors of the horse stables, sheep-folds and cattle barns are securely bolted, and women particularly are kept out lest the forces of evil use them as a vehicle for entry. In Czechoslovakia pine resin is burned throughout the nights from Christmas until New Year's, its pungent smoke driving away evil spirits; on Christmas Eve and again on New Year's Eve, shots are fired into the trees and meadows and straw is wrapped around the fruit trees to keep them away.

In various parts of Scandinavia, the *juledarna*, or "Christmas Fire," in the form of Christmas candles, torches, and hearth fire, protect against Satanic influences abroad during the holiday season. Immediately before the evening meal on Christmas Eve, a great fire is built on the hearth, to burn during dinner. Candles are burned throughout that night; early on Christmas morning additional candles are lighted and placed at the windows, while torches are placed in the yard and left burning there until the family go to early Mass. As late as the 1860's torches were burned in a circle about the church during the early Mass on Christmas morning.

In the west provinces of Sweden the farmer slaughters a lamb and while the blood flows, he says: "As the blood of Christ flowed for human beings, so may this blood flow for my cattle, to protect them against all evil that can come through the sorcery of Satan." Farm animals are rubbed with the Christmas ale— "angel's ale" or "angel's wine"—to protect them against the evil powers. In some places the horns of oxen are polished with it and the cows' hay is sprinkled with it.

In the province of Dalecarlia, in central Sweden, the cattle are fed leavened bread during the night before Christmas. Other means are employed elsewhere in Sweden to ward off evil forces from the cattle: the cows' teeth are brushed with salt and soda; salt is scattered about the cowbarns and over the animals; ashes are rubbed on the cows on Christmas day as protection against "evil bite." In Jämtland province a special dough is prepared at Christmas Eve; it contains hair of all colors from the livestock, three kernels of barley, fourteen kernels each of rye and peas, a little milk, flour, ashes, and grains of coarse salt. Between six and twelve o'clock this mixture is passed three times, in a counter-clockwise direction, over the animals to protect them from evil.

Noise is also helpful in warding off the evil spirits. On some Swedish farms, the yeast is put in the Christmas ale to the accompaniment of much loud hurrahing and shouting to discourage the forces of evil from interfering with the effective working of the yeast. For the trip to and from church early on Christmas morning bells, chimney dampers and similar noisemakers are tied to the horses. In Norway on Christmas

Eve there is much firing of guns and exploding of gunpowder for the same general purpose.

The Cross is, understandably, considered to be one of the most effective instruments for thwarting Satan and his helpers, and it is employed widely throughout Scandinavia during the Christmas season. Crosses appear over barn doors and windows, at the well, in the fields, on and around the manure piles by the barns, on the threshold of the barn, and in the ceiling of the barn above each of the animals.

A formidable underworld of malevolent sprites awakens from its slumbers at Christmas to plague the general population. The malicious *Dödingarna*, or "spirits of the dead," arise from their graves on Christmas Eve to soothe their restless spirits at the expense of the living. In Iceland, where they are especially active on Christmas morning, churchgoers protect themselves by wearing something new to church. Among the Swedes of Finland the *dödingarna* cannot speak unless spoken to first; however, one who wishes to can employ them for his own dark designs against an enemy by using bones or dirt from the graveyard as his talisman. The Finnish Swedes also fear the *Underbyggarna*, "those that build underneath," who, though small in stature, possess great power and become vengeful at the slightest offense. Ale or coffee is poured through cracks in the floor of the house as a peace offering to the *underbyggarna* at Christmas. The latter have their counterpart in the Danish *Under-jordiske*, "those under the earth," who are also quick to anger. On Christmas Eve they share in the food for the dogs and cats, and the master must be careful in feeding his pets not to utter the animals' names, lest

the *underjordiske* take offense at this implied exclusion
of themselves and wreak vengeance on their reluctant
hosts.

In Teutonic mythology the troll is a supernatural
being, conceived sometimes as a dwarf, sometimes as
a giant, and believed to inhabit caves or live in the
hills. At Christmas, in addition to locking barns, firing
shots, wrapping straw about fruit trees and decorating
the barn with crosses, the Scandinavians employ other
devices to ward off the trolls. In Borga, Finland, at
five in the morning on Christmas Eve, the farmer
attaches cowbells and other noise-makers to the
harness of the horse and rides into the meadows to
frighten away the trolls who occupy the haymows. The
Danish milkmaid performing her duties on Christmas
Eve must be careful not to snap her fingers lest a troll
hear the noise and make the cows' udders very sensitive. In Norway an axe is driven into the wall of the
cowbarn so that it will fall on the head of any troll who
tries to enter. In Sweden the wooden Christmas dove—
Bjorksvamp—hangs from the ceiling as protection
against trolls. In the Åland Islands the shutters of the
house are closed and covered with horse-blankets on
Christmas Eve, and strangers are not allowed in; a
stranger brings "troll troubles." If a stranger should
gain entry, after he has left one must throw hot ashes
after him and spit three times. Nor may one call at
another's home on Christmas day; a person who does
so is dubbed a "Christmas swine" and is given the
slop jar or the broom to sit on.

Witches roam the Swedish countryside at Christmas
Eve, their wild rides often carrying them all the way
to Stockholm. In Örebro, during the evening meal,

pieces of each kind of food are tossed into a square basket under the table. At three o'clock on Christmas morning the contents are distributed among the cattle to protect them against the witches. A small cross of rye straw attached to the ceiling of the cowbarn serves the same purpose in Vestergötland, while in Dalecarlia an axe is thrown over the roof of the cowbarn. In Denmark scissors are placed in the oats intended for the geese; the livestock are protected by fastening a little of the dough from the Christmas bread above the barn door. In Norway, a wide variety of precautions are taken: steel is fastened about the cows and horses, or put at the places where they drink and eat; brooms of juniper twigs are set up on each side of the barn door; scissors are placed above the cows; an auger is placed in the hay; a knife is thrown over the barn; an axe with its edge turned outward is put just inside the barn door; a broom and shovel are placed outside the barn door; and in some cases, the animals are fed Christmas food, whiskey and ale on the morning of Christmas day.

In the West Highlands of Scotland they burn the Old Woman of Christmas—*Gailleach Nollich*, or *Nollaig*. On Christmas Eve the head of the house goes into the woods, cuts down a tree stump, carves it into the semblance of an old woman, brings it home and burns it in the center of the room. When the Old Woman is reduced to ashes, the Christmas festivities formally begin. In some localities of Scotland this pagan ceremony propitiates the angel of death who will then stay away from the house during the coming year.

In Macedonia, during the twelve-day period from the Nativity to Epiphany (December 25 to January 6), certain persons possessed of a special "light" are transformed by night into fearful and dreaded monsters called *Karkantzari*. During the three great feasts which fall in this period, special efforts are made to neutralize the evil powers of these malevolent creatures. Their effigies are burned on Christmas Eve; on New Year's Eve they are scalded; and on Epiphany Eve faggots are lighted on the hearth to consume the *karkantzari* lurking beneath the ashes.

In Swiss legend, St. Christopher's treasure—a pot full of gold coins—was secreted in a cave; there it was guarded by one of the Devil's minions, in the form of a magnificent male goat, with horns outspread like the wings of a griffin in full flight. Its eyes were a bright red, its foul stench kept people away, and it never slept. Once a year, during the Christmas Eve midnight Mass, this creature left its post at the cave, leaving the treasure unguarded. One Christmas Eve three men sneaked into the cave, raised the flagstone from the floor and found the pot of gold coins. Just as they were preparing to make off with it, the goat returned, its eyes blazing like yellow sparks and its sulphurous fumes nearly suffocating the three thieves. In a panic, the latter dashed out of the cave and threw themselves into the black abyss of the Merdenson torrent.

In Sparby, Norway, on the night of Christmas Eve, the supernatural *Bjara* is created, in the form of a rabbit or other animal, to steal dairy products for his creator the Devil. In Setesdal any animal with claw which is inside the house during the night of Christmas Eve is transformed into an evil being. In Finland the *Mara* of ancient Teutonic folklore, an incubus who sits on a sleeper's chest and produces nightmares, attacks the horses on Christmas Eve, unless the horses are given a protective rye flour which puts marrow into their bones.

The nomadic Lapp peoples of Scandinavia fear a cruel and malignant giant called Stallo, who gathers children in his sack and carries them off. On Christmas Eve Stallo travels about in a caravan drawn by small animals, generally lemmings or mice, and the ground in front of the tents must be kept free of chips and other trash, lest Stallo's team get stuck there. A plentiful supply of water must be kept in the tent because if Stallo finds no water to quench his thirst he is likely to suck the blood from the children. The children must also be careful not to use bad language or make too much noise on Christmas Eve lest Stallo kill them. In the early nineteenth century it was a custom among the Lapps of Finnmark (northern Norway) at Christmas time for three or more young men to visit the neighbors' houses and ask for the "King's tax." The strongest of the group would wrap himself in rags to impersonate Stallo; he would carry a wooden phallus with which to prod the girls and ask them to pay the "tax." In Setesdal in southern Norway the Christmas procession is known as the *Stålesferdi* and is led by a giant called *Ståle*, which in Norwegian means "a tall strong man."

CHAPTER ELEVEN

Portents and Charms

ONE of the many pagan practices, particularly in Scandinavia, which has been incorporated into the Christmas tradition, is the divining of fortunes for the coming year. This is a transfer to Christmas of an old pagan custom formerly practiced at the time of the New Year, and represents a continuation of customs in vogue when the New Year began at the winter solstice.

If an unmarried person wishes to ascertain his (or her) prospects for the forthcoming year, several methods are available. Among the Swedes of Finland, one may either abstain from all liquids on Christmas Eve, or else eat nine small herrings tail first. In either case, his or her future spouse will appear in a dream on the following night, bringing water to quench a well-developed thirst. Or, following the noon dinner on the day after Christmas, a rooster is brought into the house and placed on the floor in the center of a circle of the unmarried members of the family; in front of each is a crumb of bread. The person to whom the rooster comes first will be married during the year.

Among the Cheremis of east central Russia Christmas Eve is a time for discerning the general physical

outlines of the prospective husband or wife. At nightfall
one goes to the sheep-pen; there, in the dark, he or
she grasps a sheep by the foot. If the sheep is white,
the future spouse will be a blond (or blonde); if black,
a brunet (or brunette); if old and fat, so too the spouse;
if young, young. In Hungary on Christmas Eve, a man
who is willing to brave the cold may run naked around
the house and look through the window. If he sees many
people inside, then he will be married during the
coming year.

Matrimonial divination at Christmas time appears to
be more widespread and marked by a more complex
ritualism among girls than among boys. In Devonshire,
England, a girl goes into the yard on Christmas Eve
and raps on the door of the henhouse. If a hen cackles,
she will never marry; if a cock crows, she will marry
before the end of the coming year. Would-be brides of
Bohemia put colored candles inside the shells of the
first parcel of nuts which they open during the day.
Identifying each shell with the name of a prospective
husband, they light the candles inside and float their
small "ships" in a basin of water. He whose "ship"
first approaches the girl will be her husband; however,
the girl can manipulate her own fortunes by blowing
unwanted vessels away from her until she gets the one
she wants. But if a candle should go out in the process,
the man it represents will die within the year.

Lithuanian girls employ a technique which obviously
derives from the same source as the practice of their
counterparts of Bohemia. They write the names of
each of their prospective grooms on a piece of paper.
The names are then pasted around the border of a
dish; the dish is filled with water; a small "boat" is

floated in the dish and comes to rest in front of the name of the future husband. Lithuanian maids can also divine their marriage prospects by reading tea leaves on Christmas Eve, or by reading the verdict of the woodpile. In the latter instance, a girl picks up a load of firewood and counts the sticks; an even number of sticks forecasts a wedding during the coming year; an odd number means a convent in the girl's near future. A similar practice among the Cheremis of Russia calls for the unmarried girl to take a single piece of wood from the woodpile at dusk on Christmas Eve. A short piece foretells a short husband; a long piece, a tall one.

In Hungary a girl takes an armful of sticks to her room and puts them under her pillow, together with a petticoat turned inside out. When she awakens the following morning she counts the sticks; an even number assures her of marriage within the year. Hungarian girls also have other means of reading their marriage future. Just before midnight on Christmas Eve, a girl can see her future husband by staring, naked, into a mirror. Or she can heat the stove, stand naked on a bench in front of it, look between her legs into the stove, and see him in the glow of the fire. Or, before she goes to midnight Mass, she covers the table with a white cloth, on top of which she places a glass of water and a glass of wine. On returning from Mass, she undresses and sits naked at the table. Her future husband will then appear; if he drinks of the wine he will be a rich man; if the water, he will be poor.

Among the Swedes of Finland a girl may see her intended by sitting between two mirrors, with a light beside her, at midnight of Christmas Eve. She may also sweep the floor with her chemise, or set the table for her unknown suitor, and then go outdoors and see him there.

Equally with marriage, death is a matter of consuming interest, and it is not surprising to find that the Christmas season is also a time to divine one's prospects of an earthly future. In Scandinavia generally, on Christmas Eve a candle is placed on the table before each person. If the light of one's candle goes out, or the flame sinks, that person will due during the year. Also, during dinner on Christmas Eve, one walks three times, counter-clockwise, around the house and looks in through a window. If one of the persons inside the house appears to be headless, that person will die during the year. In Hungary the same principle prevails, with some variation in method: to find out whether or not a member of the family will die during the year, one heats the stove, runs naked three times around the house, looking through the window on each circuit. If he sees someone spread out in the middle of the room, that person is marked for death; if he sees nobody, there will be no early death in the family.

Among the Swedish communities of Finland, an extensive apparatus of divination takes on the form of a death lottery, with overtones of the ancient tradition of the Scapegoat. As in Hungary and Scandinavia generally, a person seen through the window during dinner on Christmas Eve is marked for death if he appears to be headless, or dressed in white. Also on Christmas Eve, a grain of salt is placed on the window-sill—one grain for each member of the household. The person whose grain of salt melts first will die during the year. In some areas slices of bread are used in place of salt, the disappearance of a particular slice foretelling the death of the person whom it represents. In many parts of Scandinavia, a small light above the head, or the extinguishing of the light of a candle placed on the dinner table in front of each person, signifies the demise of that person during the coming year. In Denmark, when the evening meal has been eaten and a psalm sung at the table, the family watchdog is brought in, and each member of the family throws him a piece of bread in the general area of the doorway. The person whose bread the dog takes first will "go out through the door"—that is, will die within the year.

Death omens are another pagan element incorporated in the Christmas celebrations of northern and eastern Europe. In Finland, a storm on Christmas Eve means that many prominent men will die during the year. Personal omens of death are: sneezing, arriving last at the table, turning an unbaked loaf of bread upside down, and seeing a cow lying down. A Cheremis of Russia who hears the sound of an axe on Christmas Eve will die during the year. (If he should hear the sound of threshing at the barn gate he will live throughout the year.) Elsewhere, if a burning log falls from the fireplace a member of the household will die before the next Christmas. In Czechoslovakia the natives search their houses on Christmas Eve and remove any string or linen hanging on a nail in order to forestall suicide in the family.

Other Christmas omens are somewhat less horrendous. A German who sleeps in the pigsty on Christmas day will have good luck. The Czechs carefully note who is first to enter the house at Christmas Eve: a child portends good luck; an old woman, trouble and quarreling; a girl, many men on the farm; a boy, few men on the farm. The lowing of cattle on Christmas Eve tells the Cheremis that the cattle will thrive during the coming year. If a Danish maidservant is the last to lock the door of the cowbarn on Christmas Eve, most of the calves born during the coming year will be heifers. Some of the Swedes of the west provinces believe that a dripping candle bodes sickness among the farm animals. In scattered parts of Sweden, if one goes silently to the barn on the night before Christmas, he can predict various things about his cattle on the basis of their positions in their stalls: if they stand at the side of the stall, head turned away from the cow next to them, one or more will die; if they bellow, there will be misfortune in the barn; if more than one cow is loose, bad luck generally will overtake the animals in the coming year.

The weather at Christmas time can be a a prognosis of next year's farm prosperity. In Sweden, an east wind on Christmas Eve means a high death rate among the animals. However, if the wind (from any direction) shakes the fruit trees the next year will be good for fruit. (If there is no wind to ensure a good crop, the farmer goes out and shakes the trees himself.) A cloudy sky means bad luck for the sheep and goats, provided the sky is also cloudy on St. Paul's Day. However, sunshine on the ninth day of Christmas promises good luck with the ewes and lambs. In the Reslov area, as many flies as there are at Christmas, so many lambs will there be in the spring. In Denmark, a starry sky on the thirteenth night of Christmas means that many goslings will be hatched. If it storms in Mansala (Finland) on the eleventh night of Christmas, many cattle will die. Among the Cheremis, frost on the trees at Christmas indicates a good grain crop, as does the absence of snow. If it does snow, the hazel nut crop will flourish.

The day of the week on which Christmas falls is an index to many things. An old English tradition holds that Christmas on Sunday means a good winter, windy spring, dry summer, good vineyards, plenty of honey, an abundance of sheep, and a generally peaceful year. In Lincolnshire, Christmas on Thursday forebodes much wind during the year. It is in Sweden, however, that extensive forecasts are made on this basis. If Christmas falls on:

SUNDAY: severe winter, windy spring, dry summer, dry fall. A bad year for sheep.

MONDAY: good winter, good spring, stormy summer, good fall. Pigs and cattle will do poorly.

TUESDAY: rainy winter, windy spring, rainy summer, windy fall. Bees and sheep will do poorly, as will cattle and pigs. Human mortality will also be high.

WEDNESDAY: severe winter, dry spring, dry summer, miserable fall.

THURSDAY: good winter, cold spring, good summer, rainy fall.

FRIDAY: unsettled winter, good spring, good summer, good fall. A bad year for sheep, but otherwise a year of peace and good will.

SATURDAY: miserable winter, stormy spring, dry summer, early fall. Also a bad year for sheep.

There is a considerable variety of taboos throughout Scandinavia during the Christmas season. In Gudbrandsdal (Norway), between New Year's and the twentieth day after Christmas, nothing may be made out of sheep's wool. In some parts of Sweden the cows are not watered on Christmas day lest the wolves obtain power over them; nor may one feed the pigs, or eat pigs' feet, or speak the names of the pigs; if they do, evil will certainly befall them. Knives may not be sharpened, since this will have a bad effect on the future of all the stock. If the animal dung is removed from the barn floor on Christmas day, the animals will have sore feet during the summer. If the bones of roast meat are crushed or scraped, injury will befall the legs of the living animals. The Swedes of Finland do not wash their milk-pans in the house at Christmas lest the cows' teats become sore; and they will not let the pigs out on Christmas day, for if they do the pigs will break through the fence during the following summer. If the horsebarn is cleaned in Denmark on Christmas day the best horse will die before the end of the year. The same principle applies to sheep: the sheepshed is cleaned before Christmas, and is not cleaned again until the ewes have lambed on the "Christmas manure." When the sheepshed is finally cleaned out, the task must be performed with only a shovel and pitchfork; if a broom is used the new lambs will be "swept out" too—that is, they will die.

Extensive prohibitions apply to activities which involve circular movement during the Christmas holidays. In Sweden, one who spins between Christmas and the thirteenth day thereafter, "spins [i.e., breaks] the neck of her sheep." In Finland during the same

period, spinning will inflict the sheep with *Kringejuka*
("around-sickness"), which forces the sheep to run in
a circle until they drop from exhaustion. Norwegians
do not spin on Thursday evenings during the Christmas
season because the supernatural agents abroad at that
time dislike the noise of the spinning wheel and are
likely to become unpleasant. In Denmark, if one spins
during Christmas, he will lie and "spin with his
fingers on his deathbed," and the witches and trolls
will give him no rest in the grave. In the eighteenth
century, when a Danish maid stated, before the end of
the Christmas holidays, that she wished to take out the
spinning-wheel, her mistress exclaimed: "For the
sake of the holy death of God, do not spin now. I have
only one cow, and I do not want to lose it."

On Christmas Eve, generally after sundown, the
Scandinavians ceremonially spread straw on the floor,
in memory (they say) of the newborn Savior and his
manger of straw; in some localities it is referred to
as the "bed straw of the Virgin Mary." In reality this
practice itself, as well as its many other manifestations, is a transfer to the Christian tradition of an
ancient fertility custom at the time of the winter
solstice.

The straw symbolizes the field. It is carefully
arranged on the floor to lie smooth and even, like a
carpet. Then it is sprinkled with whiskey or Christmas
ale, which represents the fructifying action of rain and
also transfers the potency of the liquors to the straw.
That night, all members of the household sleep on the
straw. Sexual intercourse between husband and wife
will have a beneficent effect on the next year's crop.
The position of the sleepers also foretells the char-

acter of the crop: if they lie straight, the grain will be strong and straight; if they lie bent or "tangled" the grain will be bent and tangled by wind and rain. If soot falls into the straw there will be "black heads" on the rye. The straw is also pitched up to the ceiling to the words: "Now I sow rye, now I sow barley" and so on, until each kind of grain is "sown"; if many straws remain stuck to the ceiling the crop will flourish.

Crosses made of the Christmas straw are placed in the fields to protect them against witches and to bestow fertility. Straw placed around the fruit trees will make them bear during the coming year. Straw burned in the cabbage garden will discourage worms on the cabbage. If it is saved and given to the horses when they are let out to pasture in the spring, they will be free from disease; if fed to setting geese, the hatch will be excellent.

In Finland, the chickens are coaxed into the house to eat their breakfast inside a straw wreath on the floor, which ensures that they will not lay their eggs away from home. In Nyland, on Christmas morning, chickens are placed inside a straw wreath, with the rooster standing in the center; if the rooster crows, eggs and chicks will be plentiful during the year. In Sweden the straw is ground into flour, from which is baked a loaf shaped like animal dung. The loaf is fed to the animals, thus preserving the fertility of the earth during the coming year.

The last sheaf of grain harvested in the fall has a special significance for the Christmas season. While a field of grain is being cut, the indwelling vital force—the spirit of vegetation—retreats before the scythe into the last stalks to be harvested. In these last

stalks, consequently, is concentrated the vital power
of the grain—the year's fruitfulness. It is then saved
until Christmas, when it is used for a variety of
purposes. A few grains from the last sheaf are mixed
with the seed grain for the next year's crop; in the
west provinces of Sweden a sheaf of pea straw is fed
to the cows on Christmas morning before church, to
ensure that the cows will keep together in the summer
pastures; in various places in Norway the sheaf is fed
to the cows, or set up outside the cowbarn; and in some
parts of Sweden small ornamental bunches are made
from the last sheaf and are hung until Christmas in the
main room of the house, after which they are cere-
moniously fed to the animals.

In the ancient myth motifs of Scandinavia and
northwest Germany, the Norse god Odin received the
last sheaf, but had to share it with the birds. So too a
sheaf of the last grain is set up for the birds at
Christmas time in Scandinavia, and although it is
considered today as an extension of the season's good
will to include animals and birds, it stems from
ancient fertility practices designed to ensure a blessing on the new year's harvest by hanging up an un-
threshed sheaf of grain for the sparrows.

The Christmas straw doll is fashioned from the last
sheaf, and is used for a variety of purposes. It is hung
up in the barns to bring good fortune to the animals.
In some parts of Sweden it is "shot" and thus the old
year's spirit of growth is killed to make way for the
coming year's spirit of fertility. It is also "pitched"
or thrown toward the ceiling—an act which apparently
symbolizes the grain goddess throwing forth the past
year's fruitfulness into the coming year. In a very old

game in Scandinavia the straw figure was set on the
floor at Christmas time; a person lying on the floor
picked up the doll with his feet, raised it over his
head and threw it forward as far as possible. If it fell
with its head toward the outside of the house, this
augured a death; the reverse position indicated that
the family would have a new member during the year.
One who succeeded in throwing it out through the
doorway would have his wish granted for the coming
year.

The area under the Christmas table has a special
sanctity and wonder-working power. A sheaf of straw
is placed under the table for the Christmas goat to lie
upon. Besides the goat, this space is also reserved for
straw crosses and the straw doll. Other objects placed
there include the drink and oats to be given to the
horses on Christmas morning, and a small quantity of
each kind of food and drink for the cattle. A vessel of
oats placed under the table on Christmas night will
ensure blessings on the coming year's crops; a
pickerel laid there will bring good luck to the next
year's fisherman. Children may romp and tumble as
they please in the straw on the floor, but they may not
play under the table. However, no matter how carefully
the floor under the table is kept clean, some kernels
of grain usually find their way there. On Christmas
Eve, or Christmas morning, one looks under the table
and reads the message of the kernels of grain, whose
positions indicate the yield of the next year's harvest.

CHAPTER TWELVE

Christmas Rituals

MANY customs associated with Christmas have their origins in practices that have nothing to do with Christianity, and in many instances, antedate Christianity itself. The celebration of a winter festival in the last week of December was practiced by the heathen Britons and also by the ancient Romans. The Roman Saturnalia, for example, was held in honor of Saturnus, the fertility god of agriculture, in mid-December, and was given over to religious ceremonies and banquets, and even included the practice of exchanging gifts. A later Roman festival in honor of the sun god Mithra was celebrated about December 25, and embodied similar practices.

In the sixth century, December 25 was celebrated in Constantinople as the birthday of *Sol Invictus*, the "unconquered sun." In some Calabrian villages of present-day Italy, peasant girls fasten ropes to iron rings in the ceiling, swing on them, and sing certain songs at Christmas time. Similarly in Cadiz, Spain, swings are put up in the courtyard of the house, or if there is not enough room for them outside, in the house itself, and the local youngsters swing and sing. The observance of this custom at Christmas—that is, at the time of the winter solstice—suggests that in

Calabria and Cadiz (as in some parts of Estonia) this pleasant pastime was originally a magic rite designed to assist the sun in climbing the steep ascent to the top of the summer sky. It is also reminiscent of the gold and the golden hair mentioned by the youths and maidens of the Greek island of Seriphos who, as they swing, refer to the "golden swing in the sky," that is, the sun, whose golden lamp swings daily across the blue vault of heaven. In Scandinavia it is believed that at Christmas time water turns to wine because, like the sun, its course is changed at that time of year. And it is a matter of interesting speculation to note that in some parts of Maryland (U.S.A.) there is a popular belief that the water in the springs turns into wine at midnight on Christmas Eve.

The Christmas tree was well known in south Germany early in the seventeenth century, where it was an outgrowth of an old German tradition symbolizing the rebirth of life after the winter solstice. The same tradition has a counterpart in Sweden. In Osterbotten, on Christmas Eve, children put up wooden "Yule crosses," which are hung with lanterns of various colors and embellished with many kinds of wooden carved ornaments prepared for the occasion and lighted on the holiday mornings and evenings. In some places the custom developed of tying pine branches at the end of a pole and attaching a stick at right angles to form a cross; elsewhere in Sweden, holes were bored at the top of the pole to receive carved wooden pegs whose adhering curling chips suggested foliage. The higher the pole the higher the rye would grow in summer.

In Germany, a green branch, or a bush, as well as the tree, symbolizes the rebirth of life after the

winter solstice, which may explain the custom of
"Easter Smacks," observed in some parts of Germany
and Austria during the Christmas holiday, and particularly on Holy Innocents Day, December 28. Young men
and women beat one another with branches of green
birch, willow, or fir, each sex having a special day for
thus whipping the other sex. In Orlagau, on the second
day of the Christmas holiday, girls beat (using fresh
green fir branches) their parents, relatives, godparents and friends. On the following day boys do the
same. During the ceremonies the children say: "Good
morning! Fresh green! Long life! You must give us a
bright Thaler," and express other similar good wishes
and requests.

It was not until the nineteenth century that the use of
the Christmas tree spread with any success beyond
Germany. It was introduced into France about 1840,
and into England the following year when the German-
born Prince Consort (Albert) brought one into Windsor
Castle. It is said that a Christmas tree was set up at
Fort Dearborn in America in 1804. However, it appears
that German influence was largely responsible for the
early use of the tree in this country. In 1833 a German
doctor in Philadelphia invited patients and friends to
come and see his lighted tree. A German family in
Cincinnati had a Christmas tree in 1845; and in 1851
a Lutheran minister in Cleveland nearly lost his church
because he set up a Christmas tree there, in the face
of local feelings that this was a pagan, unnatural form
of idolatry.

The Eastern (Orthodox) Church has not been very
receptive to the Christmas tree. In 1864, when the
then Danish Prince of Schleswig-Holstein-Sonderburg-

Glucksburg became Georgios I, King of Greece, he took with him the yuletide customs of his northern lands, including some young fir trees. The trees were set out, but did not thrive, and those that survived were largely destroyed during successive revolutions. After the return to Greece of Georgios II, the remaining trees were carefully tended, but their use as Christmas trees was prohibited for fear they might be utilized too freely after the Nordic fashion.

Christmas greens in general carry various kinds of ancient superstition with them. In Glasgow, Scotland, Christmas greens may be put up at any time, but they must be taken down before January 6. In Yorkshire, England, something green is taken into the house on Christmas morning, before anything is taken out; in Lincolnshire, it is bad luck to burn the evergreens used for Christmas decorations, and in the state of Kentucky (U.S.A.) it is bad luck to leave the Christmas greens up after New Year's day.

Mistletoe is an old pagan survival, and was held sacred by the Druids. The ancient legend of the custom of kissing under the mistletoe once inspired the following verses:

> Beneath an ancient oak, one day,
>   A holy friar kneeled to pray;
> Scarce had he mumbled Aves three
>   When lo, a voice within the tree.
> Straight to the friar's heart it went-
>   A voice as of some spirit
>   pent within the oak,
> That cried "Good Father set me free!"

Quoth he, "This hath an evil sound," and
  Bent him lower to the ground,
But ever though he prayed, the more
  The voice his pity did implore;
Until at last his eyes he raised
  And there beheld a maiden ghostly fair.
Thus to the holy friar she spoke:

"Within the hollow of the oak
  Four hundred years have I been bound.
Nor anything can break the ban
  'Til I be kissed by a holy man."

"Woe's me," then cried the friar;
  "If thou be sent to tempt me break my vow;
But whether maid or fiend thou be
  I'll stake my soul to set thee free!"

The friar then crossed himself and
kissed the maid
  When in a trice she vanished–
"Heaven forgive me now, my broken vow.
  If I have sinned, I sinned to save another
  from a living grave!"

Then down upon the earth he fell
  And prayed some sign that he might
Tell if he were doomed forever more.
  When lo, the oak all bare before
Put forth branches of palest green
  And fruited everywhere between
With waxen berries, pearly white
  A miracle, before his sight.

The friar went his way and told his tale
 And from that day it hath been writ
That any man may blameless kiss what
maid he saw
 Nor any one shall say him "No"
Beneath the holy mistletoe.

Like the mistletoe, the oak tree was also sacred to
the Druids. In the Christian Christmas tradition, the
special Yule log is frequently of oak, and is attended
with special ceremonies. In Serbia, the day before
Christmas, one of the men of the house sets out into
the woods to cut down a young oak tree. From this he
cuts the Yule log, which is carried ceremonially into
the house by the head of the family at dusk on Christmas Eve, and placed on the hearth fire. In the Poljice
region of Dalmatia on Christmas Eve three logs are
placed on the hearth, two at the bottom and one on top,
symbolizing the Holy Trinity. They are sprinkled with
holy water and a special guard is posted at night to
ensure that they will burn continually. In some villages
this fire is kept until the New Year; if it should go out
a catastrophe will befall the household in the coming
year. On Holy Innocents Day—the last of the Christmas
days—unburnt portions taken from the hearth are kept
until New Year's day. In Montenegro, until recently,
the blood of fowl, goat, or sheep was sprinkled on the
Yule log.

In Kristdala parish, Småland, Sweden, the Yule log
burns throughout the night, throwing a flickering light
over the room. It must not be dark in the house during
Christmas night, for during the night on which the
Savior was born, it never grew dark. In Gotland, after

the work of Christmas Eve is finished, a long log is brought in to be burned; the fireplace will not contain all of it, so one end is supported on a stool. The fire must not be permitted to consume all of it; a remnant is hidden away; another is thrown into the sheepshed to bring good luck with lambs. If the last remnant should be burned, out of it would fly something which resembles a bird, and the blessing would disappear from the farm.

The Yule log—*la bûche de Noël*—is traditional all through France. In Provence, it is cut from an apple tree, and its ashes have many virtues. As late as the early 19th century the entire family brought in the log, carrying it single-file with the oldest member of the family on one end and the youngest on the other. It was taken three times around the kitchen, was sprinkled with wine, placed on the andirons and lighted.

In Burgundy, when the huge Yule log is placed on the fire on Christmas Eve, the family solemnly sing Christmas carols. The father sends the smallest child into a corner to pray that the Yule log may bear sugar-plums; meanwhile, elders place little parcels of sweets under the log for the children, who believe that the sweets were borne by the log itself.

In some places much importance is attached to the Christmas candle, a reminder of the birth of the Savior, the "light of the world." In many localities of Ireland, for example, lighting the Christmas candle is one of the most important duties of that season; in County Mayo a candle burns at the window throughout the night and is not extinguished until it burns itself out.

In Norway, Christmas candles are moulded large enough to last throughout the holiday season. "Sinful hands'' are not allowed to touch it during Christmas Eve. On Christmas morning the remnants are put into a lantern and are used to singe the tail, or the right side, of each cow. Stubs of the Christmas candles are also melted and fed to the bull, in order to make him vigorous. In Denmark the stubs of Christmas candles are saved for medicinal use on sick farm animals, and in Vestmanland (Sweden) the cows' udders are rubbed with Christmas candles to prevent chapping. In Finland, if a calf is born during the day before Christmas an extinguished candle is passed around the cow and her teats to ensure good luck with the calves. And in many sections of the Pyrenees the Candlemas candle, kept lighted during a storm, is a protection against thunder, lightning and hail.

Beyond Europe, the Christmas celebration has also been shaped by local customs. In some districts of western Maryland, at a children's party the mother ''switches'' the Christmas tree with a small stick. As the goodies fall to the ground, the children scramble for them. Sometimes they dance around the tree, to music, singing: ''Here we go round the Christmas tree''—presumably, to the tune of ''Here we go round the mulberry bush.'' Suddenly the dance stops, and each child is given a candy cane, a bag of candy, or other gift. Coals may not be taken into the house on Christmas day. The Christmas log is dipped into a stream, to make it last longer. He who eats no beans on this day will become an ass. Plum pudding is eaten, because the Wise Men brought spices to Jesus. In some families in Baltimore, the children thoughtfully place a pillow in the chimney so that Santa Claus may alight in comfort. Christmas decorations are forbidden in upper rooms.

Throughout the southern United States, from Maryland to Texas, Christmas is celebrated by exploding firecrackers; north of the Mason and Dixon line this is not done. In Tennessee in the early nineteenth century, Davey Crockett used to fire salutes with his rifle, sing his merriest songs, tell his funniest stories, and indulge himself with copious quantities of whiskey in celebration of Christmas.

In some sections of the Virginia Alleghanies, the custom of bellsniggling still prevails. About a week before Christmas, men in women's clothes, and women in men's clothes, their faces concealed by homemade masks, go to the door of each house and the occupants are challenged to identify them. Handouts are expected. The custom is a transfer of a performance on Beggars' Night, before Hallowe'en. *Bellsniggle* is derived from Palatinate German *Belschnickel*, or *Belsh Nichel*—that is, Santa Claus.

Pennsylvania Germans were familiar with the figure of Belsnickel, known as Knecht Ruprecht in Germany. He was supposed to be a servant of St. Nicholas, who punished bad children and rewarded good ones with presents. It appears that the servant in this case has merged with the master, St. Nicholas.

Among the aboriginal peoples of America, many Christmas practices have been blended with native traditions. The Christmas and New Year dances which the Eskimo now perform at Point Barrow, Alaska, follow an old native Messenger Feast pattern. The midwinter celebration of the Upper Tanana natives of Alaska, at which gifts were exchanged, provided an easy transition to the Christmas celebration, with its gift-giving.

On the Washington Yakima reservation the Indians adapted Christmas to their native potlatch and longhouse ceremonies. At their gatherings, the native chants and dances alternate with Christmas carols, the ceremonies often lasting from Christmas until the New Year.

The Yurok of northern California rejected the Christmas tree because it suggested to them the fir shrubs which they erected beside persons under taboo because they had handled a corpse. The Eastern Dakota call Santa Claus *Wa zi ya*, their designation of the giant in the north who blows out the cold air.

At the Cochiti pueblo in the southwestern United States, a Catholic priest attempted to prevent the performance of native dances as part of the Christian celebration. There was much opposition to this, the natives declaring that he had no right to interfere in such matters, it being his function to supervise the Mass and not to interfere with local custom.

At the Isleta pueblo of New Mexico, during the four days from December 25 to 28, there is dancing in front of the church. On Christmas night men and women dance inside the church, in two alternating groups. At the Jemez pueblo, dough images of domestic animals are made at Christmas and are buried in corrals. Near the church ruin, dough crosses are buried in a hole into which corn meal was sprinkled—a modification of aboriginal custom.

At Acoma, after midnight on Christmas Eve many people take into the church, in baskets or bowls, small clay images of horses, cattle, sheep, corn and other things. They place them on the floor and pray to God, Jesus, and their patron saint, San Estevan. A cross, placed in a bowl for God, ensures a generous increase of livestock and crops during the year. The images remain in the church for four days; they are then deposited in the fields, at the base of cedar bushes or in rock fissures. At sunrise the people dance. During the following four days there is much dancing in the church, where they perform the Buffalo, Eagle, and other dances but do not, as on other occasions, wear masks.

At the Santa Ana pueblo, the Christmas celebration lasts four days—from Christmas Eve until the evening of December 28—four being a ritual number among some of the southwestern tribes of the United States. On Christmas Eve the sacristan brings out a small image of Jesus, about eight inches long, and displays it on a platform in front of the church altar. The natives bring to the church small unbaked clay images of domestic and game animals, some corn, melons and other goods, and place them in front of the altar, thus ensuring the power and blessings of Jesus on the game, herds and crops.

In Tikopia, a Polynesian island in the Solomons, the institution of bond-friends giving presents has partially been transferred to Christmas by the Christianized natives. These gifts, which now take the form of Christmas presents, were formerly exchanged in the monsoon season, after the cycle of ceremonies known as the "Work of the Gods," which was held at about the same time of year as our Christmas.

Western influence in Japan brought certain Christmas practices with it. Early in this century (by 1909) the custom-house department was observing December 25 as a holiday, for the "accommodation of foreign employees.'' By 1930 children in Japan were observing Christmas and its celebration was becoming popular. Father Christmas began to appear in effigy everywhere, and Christmas day dinners, with turkey and plum-pudding, became standard restaurant fare. Santa Claus would make his entry through the sliding-door of the house, there being no chimney in the Japanese home; stockings were laid on the floor by the head of the sleeping mat, for there was no bedstead or mantle to accommodate them.

However, there has been some opposition on the part of the Japanese to the Christmas tradition. In 1934, when a leading foreign-style hotel, owned and operated by Japanese, was preparing for its annual Christmas Eve dinner dance and party, representatives of four Japanese patriotic societies protested to the management that the Christmas celebration was a Western importation, and they threatened to break up the proceedings. In more recent years (1948), in deference to Buddhist protests, Christmas decorations were removed from some twenty Tokyo railway stations. Nevertheless, the traditionalists have been unable to stem the enthusiasm of the Japanese children and the Japanese merchants for this Western importation.

The West itself has seen recently a few ''patriotic'' efforts to abolish or modify Christmas along more nationalistic lines. In the 1930's the Nazis rejected the Bethlehem story, including the three wise men and the Christ child in the manger. They accused Christianity of taking the Winter solstice tradition from ancient Germany and converting it into a world celebration of a religion based on the Jewish desert god Jehovah. The Hitler bodyguard celebrated Christmas as a Winter solstice festival in the ancient Teutonic manner, with torchlights and a huge bonfire, and appropriate exhortations from their superiors to remind them that the Germanic nation in former times yearly renewed its life at the Winter solstice, and that Christmas therefore should properly be understood as an all-embracing and unifying celebration of the whole Germanic community.

In December 1959, Fidel Castro announced to the Cuban people in a television broadcast that Santa Claus was a foreigner, and that henceforth he would be replaced by Don Feliciano ("Mr. Happiness") who, to the surprise of no-one, bears a strong resemblance to Castro himself.

CHAPTER THIRTEEN

Easter

THE role of the rabbit, or the hare, in Easter celebrations is reminiscent of ancient Egyptian concepts regarding the hare, although there is no evidence of transmission of these concepts from Egypt to Europe, and the similarity may be due to independent origins.

In pre-dynastic Egypt the hare was called *Um*, the "Springer-up," and was a form of the sun god Ra. Sometimes he bore the title *Nu-Nefer*, as a form of the god Osiris, who symbolized resurrection and the restoration of life.

In present-day Egypt the Coptic Christians celebrate the Easter season in a manner which (understandably) takes on many of the characteristics of a spring festival. On Easter Sunday the people sleep with onions, broad-beans and roses under their pillows. The following day (Easter Monday) they break the onions and fasten them to the door, along with a vessel of water. The beans are stuck to the bolt of the door. Everyone inhales the odor of the roses and also drinks in quantities of fresh air to see them through the day; for this day is the eve of the fifty-day season of terror—the *Chamasin*—which lasts until Whitsuntide (Pentecost), during which time a serpent travels over the earth, poisoning the atmosphere and causing smallpox, cholera and other dreaded ailments.

The Cheremis of Russia celebrate their Great Day holiday which begins on the Tuesday before Easter and continues through the following Tuesday. This is a time when the dead walk, spirits are abroad, and omens can be read. Food and drink are prepared for the spirits of the dead relatives; special prayers are said to the spirits of the underworld; numerous taboos are observed for the protection of the crops and the advancement of individual well-being, and omens are studied in order to ascertain one's prospects for the coming year.

Throughout Scandinavia at Easter time, as at the Christmas season, the night creatures come out to make mischief. The *Dymmeln*, or "Quiet Week," begins at noon on the Wednesday before Easter, and ends on Easter Eve. During this period, the troll women, or "Easter hags," are most active, and special precautions must be taken against them. The handles are removed from all brooms and the brooms are hidden; without brooms to ride on, these witches are partially immobilized. Crosses (generally of tar) are made on doors, granary boxes, manure piles, the inside walls of barns, the ceilings over the animal stalls, and on the outside of the barns. In Dalecarlia the church bells are silenced, because during these nights the witches scrape the metal from them; the scraping cleans the bells and makes it possible to hear them at greater distances, which enlarges the witches' sphere of activity, for at this time of the year, they are busiest and most troublesome wherever church bells can be heard.

In Vestbo, as protection against the Easter hags, a triangular wooden bowl, such as is used in making cheese, is made before sunrise, and a cross is set in the center of it. In one corner of the bottom is written, *per ipsum*; in another corner, *cum ipsum*; in the third corner, *in ipsum omavia*. The cows are then milked, after which the farmer's wife locks herself in the house, makes a little cheese in the bowl, puts the cheese over live coals, and recites the Lord's Prayer three times, while the cheese burns up on the coals. At this point, a woman impersonating a troll comes to the door of the house and asks permission to enter on the pretext that she wishes to borrow something. She is refused admittance and receives nothing. This treatment renders the troll harmless.

In Iceland on Shrove Thursday witches ride to a mountain called *Räckelfjäil*. As protection against them an axe is placed on the manure pile and a knife is driven in over the doors of the horsebarn. Knives and scissors are also placed in the feed bins, and in some instances needles are stuck into the wings of the fowl.

In Borga parish, Finland, knives and sickles are driven into the ceiling of the barn to prevent the *Maran* from riding the animals during the night. One of the more courageous residents of the farm sits on the roof; when the trolls come at midnight they will not be able to enter. In the morning the only unusual thing about will be a heap of ashes outside the door. The cows inside will be safe and sound.

In Edelskog, Vermland (Sweden), on the evening before Easter the backs of the cows and the foreheads of the sheep are tarred to protect them against trolls. The Finns of central Sweden fire a gun and utter the name of a hag. If it is the correct name, the hag will fall and break a thighbone. In Sweden, Norway and Denmark one must not build an early fire on Easter day; the first person to have smoke rising from his chimney will give the trolls power during the year to harm the animals on his farm.

Easter in Scandinavia is also a time for providing safeguards for the animals against a wide variety of troubles. In the Åland Islands a shepherd's horn is blown in the mountains, to protect the flock against wild animals. In Angermanland, on the evening before Easter a horn is blown at the entrance to the barn; as far as the sound carries, so far will wild animals remain away during the year. In Warend, on the wooden latch of the door of a new barn, or on the flap of the animal's collar, a cross is carved as protection against evil in general. Also, some of the food prepared for Shrove Tuesday is saved for the cattle and is given to them when they are let out to pasture in the spring. This ensures that they will come home in proper style and without mishap.

In Norway, chopping with an axe is not permitted on Shrove Thursday; if chips fly over the creatures, they will be sick; if they step on the chips, they will be lame. In Norway and Denmark, before eating on Easter day, one should bite three times a small stone and each time say, slowly: "Bears, wolves, and other wild animals shall have no more meat from my animals this year than I have had from this stone." The harder one bites the more effective the formula.

In Sweden, if a farmer eats eggs on the day before Easter, the livestock will run about in the summer pastures like "giddy hens." In Östergötland, to protect

cattle against disease, before sunrise on Easter day a
woman, when she goes to the barn to feed them, drapes
a red skirt about her shoulders, passes armfuls of
hay up inside the skirt, and three times throws some
of the hay down before each animal.

Several centuries ago, in the Rhineland, the clergy
had the privilege of collecting eggs from parishioners
during Lent. Because of the diligence and zeal with
which the privilege was exercised, it was popularly
known as *Eierdreschen*, "egg-threshing." In Paris,
children are told that, after Palm Sunday Masses,
the bells of the church of St. Germain l'Auxerrois in
that city fly to Rome; on Holy Saturday they fly back to
announce the Resurrection, and to scatter Easter eggs
in the gardens.

In Spain, Easter celebrations continue throughout
Holy Week, from Palm Sunday through Easter Sunday.
Palm fronds, made into various forms as garlands,
are sold extensively. After one of these has been
blessed, if the spray is burned a small portion at a
time it will protect the house against destructive wind
and lightning. (The village poor use laurel and rose-
mary, or olive branches.) On Easter Sunday godparents
give their godchildren a pastry in which one or more
eggs are mixed—sometimes as many eggs as the
birthdays the child has celebrated. The top of the
pastry is encrusted and the pastry is baked, shells
included. This gift is designated by the Arabic word
Muna, "provisions." Easter eggs are sometimes
colored, though not as commonly as in most other
European countries.

In Scotland, egg-rolling on Easter Sunday and
Monday is a common custom. At the end of the last

century, boys used to steal as many eggs as they
could and hide them until Easter Sunday. On that
day they would retrieve their eggs and go to some
secluded spot where they were not likely to be dis-
turbed, to feast on them. Only stolen eggs were
proper fare for the occasion.

As is the case with Christmas and other Christian
celebrations the Indians of the New World have
blended many of their ancient pagan practices into
the traditional festivals of their newly adopted faith.
During the Easter celebration at Santa Ana pueblo in
New Mexico, the people are summoned to the church.
The men take their weapons; the guns they lean near
the door, against the wall; other weapons—bows,
arrows, shields and clubs—they lay on the floor.
During the service, when the sacristan rings the
altar bell, the men turn their guns muzzle-end down,
and the shields face up. Two men, with guns, stand
guard over the large crucifix which, after the service,
is placed on the floor in front of the altar. The guard
is changed every hour and a half, until the afternoon
service, and is then discontinued. Only on the following
Saturday, after the service has ended, may the church
bell be rung. Meanwhile its function is performed by
a wooden clapper or a rattle. Only necessary work,
such as cooking or feeding and watering the horses,
is permitted. In the houses cloths are put over the
pictures of Christ and the saints. Usually a masked
katcina dance is held on Thursday or Friday, or on
both days. On Thursday, if there is no masked dance,
after the morning service the men sit in front of the
church and play games, such as ''horse race,'' dice,
or lots. The women take food to the church and leave

it in front of the altar. Both the men and the women also place lighted candles there.

At the Isleta pueblo on Easter Sunday small boys, their backs painted with figures of a chicken hawk, rabbit, or turtle, hold races. In a year in which the Scalp Ceremony is performed, contestants in the race ask the Scalps and the Sun to help them. At Zuni the final rites include flagellation, and are performed on the third day of the full moon after the spring solstice, which frequently falls at about the same time as the Christian Easter. The Penitentes of New Mexico carry out their flagellation rites on Good Friday, often with an enthusiasm and realism which disconcerts the non-Indian population. In some Mexican villages, on Holy Saturday, boys are whipped in the church to "make them grow."

Conclusion

THROUGH all periods of history there has been incessant change in human affairs. This applies to so-called established institutions, customs, traditions, ethical standards, and values, no less than to the obviously ephemeral.

Nothing that does not change lives long; in fact, it does not live at all, for the absence of change is death. Even death involves change, though a change not dynamically directed by the defunct organism.

We write our national Constitution to ensure that its content be manifest and explicit; and then we wisely provide for amendments to it. The meanings of the Constitution and its amendments are not as unchanging as the document which embodies them. As Chief Justice Hughes reminded us: "We are governed by the Constitution, and the Constitution is what the Supreme Court says it is."

Supreme Courts have said different, and sometimes contradictory, things about the meaning of some explicit statements in the Constitution. The "Supreme Court" itself is actually a succession of Supreme Courts. The pliability of the Constitution, and the adaptability of Supreme Courts have made it possible for that document of 1787 to survive as a guiding instrument of government from pre-industrial times into an atomic age; from a government by property-owning white males to one in which women—the property-less—and to some extent all races, have the franchise.

Another written document—the New Testament—has been variously interpreted through the centuries. In each century it has been diversely understood by those who accepted it as a source of religious inspiration and guidance. A variety of sects, or cults, have appeared, each possessed of the certain conviction that its adherents are following the fundamental and most important directives embodied in that document. Some, perhaps all, of the more important of these cults have been influenced by practices and concepts foreign to the New Testament, particularly from other cultures with which they have had contacts, direct or indirect.

Each cult is to some degree a creature of its own time and place; it uses the language of its social milieu, and embodies some current concepts and values. But each cult is also a product of other times and places—that is, a product of history itself, from which it inherits concepts and values of whose origins and meaning it is not entirely aware.

To be dynamic, a cult must change. The pages of this book contain only a minute portion of the story of the flow of Christianity in various channels, and the illustrations here brought to the attention of the reader may not even be the most significant part of the story. But a part of the story they are, though no part is a finished chapter.

We stand on the threshold of things to come, of whose specific character we are, of (perhaps happy) necessity, quite ignorant. Of one thing we may be assured: the story of the next hundred years will not be a repetition of the story of any preceding century. Nor will any cult which flourishes at the present day be the same a century hence.

Selected Bibliography

Aall, Lilly W. *Juletreet i Norge* (The Christmas Tree in Norway). Oslo, 1953.

Afoldi, A. *The Conversion of Constantine and Pagan Rome*. New York, 1949.

Andrew, Emily J. "Two Christmas Eve Customs." *Folklore*, 6 (1895): 93.

Anesake, Mahaharu. *History of Japanese Religion with Special Reference to the Social and Moral Life of the Nation*. London, 1930.

Angus, Samuel. *The Mystery Religions and Christianity.*

Äring, Årets. *Etnologiska Studier i Skördes och Julens Tro och Sed*. (The Year's Crop. Ethnological Research into Traditions at Harvest-time and Christmas). Stockholm, 1947.

Ausubel, Nathan (ed.). *A Treasury of Jewish Folklore*. New York, 1948.

Barnett, Homer G. *Innovation: The Basis of Cultural Change*. New York, 1953.

Barnett, James H. *The American Christmas: a Study in National Character.* New York, 1956.

Bavinck, J. H. *An Introduction to the Science of Missions.* Philadelphia, 1960.

Bevan, Edwyn. *Christianity.* New York, 1932.

Beza, Marcu. *Paganism in Roumanian Folklore.* New York, 1928.

Billson, Charles J. "The Easter Hare." *Folklore,* 3 (1892): 441.

Bird, Isabella L. *Unbeaten Tracks in Japan.* New York, 1880.

Briggs, John E. "The Iten Christmas Display." *The Palimpsest* (Iowa City, Iowa), 16 (1935): 389.

Buday, George. *The Story of the Christmas Card.* London, 1951.

Budge, E. A. Wallis. *George of Lydda.* London, 1930.

Bultmann, Rudolf. *Primitive Christianity in its Contemporary Setting.* New York, 1956.

Campbell, John G. *Witchcraft and Second Sight in the Highlands and Islands of Scotland.* Glasgow, 1902.

Case, Shirley J. *The Evolution of Early Christianity. A Genetic Study of First-Century Christianity in Relation to its Religious Environment.* Chicago, 1923.

Case, Shirley J. *The Origins of Christian Super-naturalism*. Chicago, 1946.

----------. *The Social Origins of Christianity*. Chicago, 1927.

Conybeare, Frederick C. *Myth, Magic, and Morals*. London, 1909.

Collinder, Björn. *The Lapps*. Princeton, 1949.

Cope, Gilbert. *Symbolism in the Bible and the Church*. New York, 1959.

Count, Earl W. *4,000 Years of Christmas*. New York, 1948.

Cronin, Vincent. *The Wise Man from the West*. Garden City (New York), 1957.

Cyriax, A. Kellgren. "Swedish Christmas Customs." *Folklore*, 34 (1923): 314.

Daniel, G. E. (ed.). *Myth or Legend?* New York, 1956.

Davies, J. G. *The Origin and Development of Early Christian Church Architecture*. London, 1952.

Davies, J. Merle. *The Economic and Social Environment of the Younger Churches*. Calcutta, 1938.

Dawson, F. W. *Christmas: its Origins and Associations*. London, 1902.

Delehaye, H. *Les legendes grecques des saints mili-taires*. Paris, 1909.

Dexter, Thomas F., and Henry. *Cornish Crosses, Christian and Pagan*. New York, 1938.

Dubois, Abbé J. A. *Hindu Manners, Customs and Cere-monies*. Oxford, 1936.

Edwards, Charles. *The History and Poetry of Finger-rings*. New York, 1880.

Evans, E. P. *Animal Symbolism in Ecclesiastical Architecture*. London, 1896.

Faye, Paul Louis. "Christmas Fiestas of the Cupeño." *American Anthropologist*, 30 (1928): 651.

Federau, Harold W. "Planting the Church in Congo, and the Emerging Situation Today." *Practical Anthropology*, 8 (1961): 25.

Ferguson, George. *Signs and Symbols in Christian Art*. New York, 1954.

Finegan, Jack. *Light from the Ancient Past: the Archeological Background of the Hebrew - Christian Religion*. Princeton, 1946.

Forde, Daryll, and others. *Missionary Statesmanship in Africa: a Present Demand upon the Christian Movement*. Hartford, 1953.

Foster, George M., and Gabriel Ospina. "Empire's Children: the People of Tzintzuntzan." Smithsonian Institution (Washington, D.C.), *Institute of Social Anthropology*, Publication No. 6 (1948): 188.

Fox, Penelope. *Tutankhamun's Treasure*. New York, 1951.

Fraunces, John M. "The Assumption of Tradition." *America*, 80 (1950): 101.

Gallagher, L. J. *The China that Was: China as Discovered by the Jesuits at the Close of the Sixteenth Century*. Milwaukee, 1942.

Golowin, Captain. *Recollections of Japan*. London, 1819.

Grant, Frederick C. *Ancient Judaism and the New Testament*. New York, 1959.

Grove, Florence. "Christmas Mummers." *Folklore*, 10 (1899): 351.

Groves, C. P. *The Planting of Christianity in Africa*. London, 1949.

Guerrard, Albert. *French Civilization*. London, 1920.

Halpern, Joel M. *A Serbian Village*. New York, 1958.

Hamilton, William. *Lectures in Metaphysics and Logic*. Edinburgh and London, 1859.

Harrison, Michael. *The Story of Christmas. Its Growth and Development from the Earliest Times.* London, 1952.

Hartland, Edwin Sidney. *The Science of Fairy Tales.* London, 1891.

Hartman, Gertrude. *Medieval Days and Ways.* New York, 1940.

Hatch, Edwin. *The Influence of Greek Ideas and Usages upon the Christian Church.* London, 1895.

Hawks, Jacquetta, and Christopher. *Prehistoric Britain.* Cambridge (Mass.), 1953.

Herskovits, Melville J. *Man and His Works.* New York, 1948.

Highet, Gilbert. *A Clerk at Oxenford.* New York, 1954.

Hodgson, M. L. "Some Notes on the Husuls." *Folklore*, 16 (1905): 53.

Hoffman, Paul. *Country Christmas: a Reminiscence.* Knoxville (Tennessee), 1938.

Hole, Christina. *Witchcraft in England.* New York, 1947.

Howard, Helen A., and Dan L. McGrath. *War Chief Joseph.* Caldwell (Idaho), 1958.

Hughes, Everett C., and Helen M. *Where People Meet*: *Racial and Ethnic Frontiers*. Glencoe (Illinois), 1952.

Hull, Eleanor. *Folklore of the British Isles*. London, 1928.

Iwado, Tamotsu. *Children's Days in Japan*. Board of Tourist Industry, Japanese Government Railways, 1936.

Jackson, Frederick J., and Kirsopp Lake. *The Beginnings of Christianity*. London, 1920.

Jahn, Raymond. *Concise Dictionary of Holidays*. New York, 1958.

Jenness, Diamond. *The People of the Twilight*. Chicago, 1959.

Johnson, W. Braucle. "Santa Claus Comes to Life." *Contemporary Review*, 140 (1931): 771.

Kamal-Nd-Din, Kiwaja. *The Sources of Christianity*. Woking (England), 1934.

Keesing, Felix M. *The South Seas in the Modern World*. New York, 1941.

Knox, Ronald. *Literary Distractions*. New York, 1958.

Kramer, Judith R., and Seymour Leventman. *Children of the Gilded Ghetto*. New Haven, 1961.

Latourette, Kenneth S. *The Expansion of Christianity*. 7 vols., London, 1949.

Lebreton, Jules. *History of the Dogma of the Trinity*. New York, 1939.

Leslie, Charles (ed.). *Anthropology of Folk Religion*. New York, 1960.

Lewis, Oscar. *The Children of Sanchez: Autobiography of a Mexican Family*. New York, 1961.

Linton, Ralph. *The Tree of Culture*. New York, 1955.

MacDonald, Malcolm. *Borneo People*. New York, 1958.

Macgregor, G. H. C., and A. C. Purdy. *Jew and Greek, Tutors unto Christ*. New York, 1936.

Male, Emile. *L'art religieux après le Çoncile de Trente*. Paris, 1951.

----------. *L'art religieux au xiii ème siècle en France*. Paris, 1910.

----------. *L'art religieux de la fin du Moyen Age en France*. Paris, 1908.

Mannhardt, S. W. *Weihnachtsblüten in Sitte und Sage*. Berlin, 1864.

Marshall, Frank H. *The Religious Backgrounds of Early Christianity*. St. Louis, 1931.

Métraux, Alfred. *Voodoo in Haiti.* New York, 1959.

Meyer, Arnold. *Das Weihnachtsfest.* Tübingen, 1913.

Mills, Lawrence. *Avesta Eschatology Compared with the Books of Daniel and Revelation.* Chicago, 1908.

----------. *Our Own Religion in Ancient Persia.* Chicago, 1913.

Morley, Sylvanus G. *The Ancient Maya.* Stanford, 1946.

Morri, Yasotaro. *Sunrise Synthesis.* Tokyo, 1935.

Moss, Leonard W., and Stephen C. Cappannari. "The Black Madonna: an Example of Culture Borrowing." *Scientific Monthly*, 76 (1953): 319.

Murgoci, Agnes. "Roumanian Easter Eggs." *Folklore*, 20 (1909): 295.

Murray, Gilbert. *Five Stages of Greek Religion.* New York, 1925.

----------. "The Christian Tradition." *Saturday Review*, 36 (1953): 17.

Nida, Eugene A. "Mariology in Latin America." *Practical Anthropology*, 4 (1957): 69.

----------.*Message and Mission: The Communication of the Christian Faith.* New York, 1961.

Nielen, Josef M. *The Earliest Christian Liturgy*. St. Louis, 1941.

Nilsson, Martin P. "Studien zur Vorgeschichte des Weihnachtsfestes." *Archiv für Religionswissenschaft*, 19 (1918): 94.

Oliver, Douglas L. *A Solomon Island Society*. Cambridge (Mass.), 1955.

O'Malley, L. S. S. *India's Social Heritage*. Oxford, 1934.

Palanque, J. R., G. Bardy, and others. *The Church in the Christian Roman Empire*. London, 1952.

Partridge, J. B. "Folklore from Yorkshire (North Riding)." *Folklore*, 25 (1914): 375.

Peterkin, Julia. *A Plantation Christmas*. Boston, 1934.

Rahner, H. *Griechische Mythen in Christlicher Deutung*. Zurich, 1947.

Ram, B. L. Rallia. "The Caste System and Its Influence upon the Christian Church in North India." *National Christian Council Review* (November, 1938).

Rawlinson, H. G. *Intercourse between India and the Western World*. Cambridge (England), 1916.

Reed, John Paul. *Kokutai: a Study of Certain Sacred and Secular Aspects of Japanese Nationalism*. Chicago, 1940.

Reichard, Gladys A. "The Navaho and Christianity." *American Anthropologist*, 51 (1949): 66.

Scott-Moncrieff, Philip D. *Paganism and Christianity in Egypt*. Cambridge (England), 1913.

Sereno, Renzo. "Some Observations on the Santa Claus Custom." *Psychiatry*, 14 (1951): 387.

Seymour, William W. *The Cross in Tradition, History and Art*. New York and London, 1898.

Seznec, Jean. *The Survival of the Pagan Gods*. New York, 1953.

Simson, Otto G. von. "The Bamberg Rider." *Review of Religion*, 4 (1940): 257.

Spencer, Robert F. "The North Alaskan Eskimo." Bureau of American Ethnology, Bulletin 171 (1959): 378.

Swift, Emerson H. *Roman Sources of Christian Art*. New York, 1951.

Thrupp, Sylvia L. (ed.). *Millenial Dreams in Action*. The Hague, 1962.

Tille, Alexander. "German Christmas and the Christmas Tree." *Folklore*, 3 (1892): 166.

Toor, Frances. *A Treasury of Mexican Folkways*. New York, 1947.

Trevor-Roper, H. R. *Men and Events.* New York, 1957.

Underhill, Ruth M. *Papago Indian Religion.* New York, 1946.

Watts, Alan W. *Easter: Its Story and Meaning.* New York, 1949.

Weigall, Arthur. *The Paganism in Our Christianity.* New York, 1928.

Wheeler, Joseph M. *Paganism in Christian Festivals.* London, 1932.

White, Leslie A. "The Pueblo of Santa Ana, New Mexico." American Anthropological Association, *Memoirs*, 60 (1942): 267.

Wilson, Edmund. *The Scrolls from the Dead Sea.* New York, 1956.

Wisdom, Charles. *The Chorti Indians of Guatemala.* Chicago, 1940.

Yarker, J. *The Arcane Schools.* Belfast, 1909.